Praise for *Learners Without Borders*

"Yong Zhao, one of our most consistently profound leaders in the transformation of education, breaks the rigid mold of traditional schools, replacing it with a global ecosystem of student-engaged learning. In this future, which is already here, students, teachers, and a community of resources are liberated from those molds, and we are inspired to re-create school as unbounded learning environments."

Grant Lichtman, Educator, Chief Provocateur
Author, *Thrive*
Poway, CA

"This book presents some very provocative notions on why we need significant changes in today's schools. The remote learning environments that have been implemented as a result of COVID have taught us some very real lessons and this book begins to put them in the perspective of individualized and personalized learning for students at all levels."

Marianne Lescher, Principal
Kyrene Traditional Academy
Gilbert, AZ

"*Learners Without Borders* is a thought-provoking look at the opportunity before us. For decades, schools have remained relatively unchanged, though overnight change was forced upon us by a global pandemic. Zhao urges us to consider this upheaval as a gateway to fundamentally redesign schools, break the "default view" and disrupt education as we knew it."

Melissa J. Weatherwax, K–12 Instructional Technology
Averill Park Central School District

"Professor Zhao consistently pushes us to dream big about what's possible in teaching and learning. Anyone who wants a pulse on the future of our rapidly changing world needs a copy of this book!"

Julie Stern, Learning Facilitator Author,
Learning That Transfers, *Visible Learning for Social Studies*, and *Tools for Teaching Conceptual Understanding*

D1496230

"Long before COVID, a second virus began spreading around the world, infecting school systems and rendering them resistant to change. Its costs to students, families, and societies have likewise been enormous. In *Learners Without Borders*, Dr. Yong Zhao delivers the much-awaited vaccine. Its active ingredients include treating students as owners of their own learning and helping them harness technology for education, work, and life. As educators and policymakers plan for a post-COVID world, this book is their best vaccination against the pandemic of educational mediocrity."

Milton Chen, Executive Director
Emeritus, George Lucas Educational Foundation

Learners Without Borders

New Learning Pathways for All Students

Yong Zhao

FOR INFORMATION:

Corwin

A SAGE Company

2455 Teller Road

Thousand Oaks, California 91320

(800) 233-9936

www.corwin.com

SAGE Publications Ltd.

1 Oliver's Yard

55 City Road

London EC1Y 1SP

United Kingdom

SAGE Publications India Pvt. Ltd.

B 1/I 1 Mohan Cooperative Industrial Area

Mathura Road, New Delhi 110 044

India

SAGE Publications Asia-Pacific Pte. Ltd.

18 Cross Street #10-10/11/12

China Square Central

Singapore 048423

Printed in the United States of America

ISBN: 978-1-5063-7735-3

President: Mike Soules

Associate Vice President and

 Editorial Director: Monica Eckman

Senior Acquisitions Editor: Ariel Curry

Senior Development Editor: Desirée A. Bartlett

Senior Editorial Assistant: Caroline Timmings

Production Editor: Natasha Tiwari, Megha Negi

Copy Editor: Will DeRooy

Typesetter: Hurix Digital

Proofreader: Jeff Bryant

Indexer: Integra

Cover Designer: Candice Harman

Marketing Manager: Morgan Fox

This book is printed on acid-free paper.

21 22 23 24 25 10 9 8 7 6 5 4 3 2 1

Table of Contents

About the Author

Yong Zhao is a Foundation Distinguished Professor in the School of Education at the University of Kansas and a professor in educational leadership at the Melbourne Graduate School of Education in Australia. He previously served as the presidential chair, associate dean, and director of the Institute for Global and Online Education in the College of Education, University of Oregon, where he was also a professor in the Department of Educational Measurement, Policy, and Leadership. Prior to that, he was a University Distinguished Professor at the College of Education, Michigan State University, where he also served as the founding director of the Center for Teaching and Technology and executive director of the Confucius Institute, as well as the U.S.-China Center for Research on Educational Excellence. He is an elected member of the National Academy of Education and a fellow of the International Academy of Education.

CHAPTER 1

New Possibilities

It may surprise you to learn that teenagers in Nepal are using massive open online courses (MOOCs) to learn English and Egyptian, study dinosaurs, and take high-level STEM courses. On Episode 33 of *Silver Linings for Learning*, a weekly online show hosted by me and four other professors discussing educational innovations during the COVID-19 pandemic, we had five Nepalese students and two teachers as guests. They told an unexpected story of learning beyond the limits of their impoverished, rural schools. Nepal, a very small country largely located in the Himalayas, has a population of about 28 million. Nepal is not a wealthy country; with a nominal GDP of just above $1,000 in 2019, the country ranks about 159th in the world. But in this poor and remote country, teenagers have started learning from MOOCs offered by universities and other providers in the United States and other places.

In fluent English, the Nepalese students told wonderful stories of their experiences taking forty to seventy MOOCs over the past few years. They were introduced to MOOCs and supported by Mr. Baman Kumar Ghimire and Mr. Bishwa Raj Gautam, two teachers, but their learning has been entirely self-directed. One student started with a course about dinosaurs and became so interested that she studied world history to better understand the history of dinosaurs. It was a completely new world to her, as she said on the show. The students were nervous when they first started taking MOOCs, because they did not know what they would encounter. They had to manage their time because they also had regular school to attend. They had to convince their parents with their certificates that they were doing something meaningful outside of their own school.

The results are amazing. Beyond just the content these students learned in the online courses, they also learned to be independent. They learned that there was a world beyond their classrooms. They learned that they could have access to that world and participate in it. (You can watch this episode of *Silver Lining for Learning* and other videos by going to http://bit.ly/learnerswithoutborders.)

This is not to say that MOOCs are the only way for students to have access to an outside world or that MOOCs work for everyone. The message is that students, however young, can learn anything from outside their school. Today, we have MOOCs and YouTube. We have Google and Facebook. We have Khan Academy and many other courses online. We have the local community and local experts. Not one works for all, but each and every student can become owners of their learning by accessing these rich resources. They can learn beyond what is prescribed for them by a government or an educational system. They can learn without being directly taught by a teacher in their local situation.

THE FAILURE OF EDUCATIONAL REFORMS

Students have rarely been considered an active and intentional partner in efforts at educational reform. The government-led and government-driven reforms over the past few decades have played with almost all the essential elements of education. They changed curricula. They tweaked assessments. They tinkered with teachers and teaching. They held school principals account-able. They experimented with class sizes. But they never touched students directly. Students have been simply the recipients of the reforms, of the massive changes that have been created for them.

The results have not been good. The desired outcomes of the reforms have been excellence and equity—excellence being higher levels of achievement by all students and equity being a closure of the achievement gaps among different groups of students. After decades of reforms, education has not achieved either of these aims. Take the National Assessment of Education Progress (NAEP), the national report card of the United States, as an example. The most basic indicators of educational quality, the assessment of math and reading, has not seen significant improvement. The 2019 reading assessment shows that, on average, American twelfth-graders did significantly worse in 2019 than in 1992, when the assessment was first given (NAEP, 2020b). The students' math performance in 2019 on average shows no difference from that in 2005 (NAEP, 2020a). The achievement gaps between Black and White students and the gaps between Hispanic students and white students remain large (Bohrnstedt, 2015; Zhao, 2016). International assessments such as the Programme for International Student Assessment, better known as PISA, and the Trends in International Mathematics and Science Study (TIMSS) have indicated no significant improvements in most educational systems' performance over the years. The performance of most educational systems essentially stayed very much the same over the past two decades (Mullis, 2016; OECD, 2019).

OUR CHANGING WORLD

In the meantime, a lot has changed over the past three decades. Today's world is drastically different from what it was in the 1990s when TIMSS and PISA took measures of the world's students' performances and national educational policies zeroed in on the achievement gaps in education. The Internet was just beginning in the 1990s, but today the world cannot exist without it. Products and services such as Google, Twitter, Facebook, YouTube, iPhones, Amazon, eBay, and TikTok have penetrated virtually every corner of the world and altered the way we live. New technologies have displaced millions of people from their jobs and created millions of new possibilities. They have ended industries and created new ones.

The technological changes have brought new expectations for our children. It has become certain that for our children to thrive in this new world—which is still being changed by emerging technologies such as artificial intelligence, big data, and nanotechnology—they have to develop new abilities and skills. These new competencies, generally referred to as "21st century skills," include new school subjects, such as financial literacy and computer coding; capabilities such as creativity and entrepreneurial thinking; skills such as critical thinking, communication, and collaboration; mindsets and attributes such as curiosity, growth mindset, and resilience; and knowledge of social and emotional well-being and physical health.

As we were struggling to improve the traditional measures of education and help students learn the new skills and abilities, COVID-19 came. This pandemic disrupted education globally in unprecedented ways. While billions of children were sent home as schools closed, a new form of learning began. Remote learning, almost overnight, became a common solution—at least for a short time, depending on which country students were in. In the various forms of remote learning, students had to adapt to however the learning opportunities were offered. Teachers, as well, had to be innovative and adaptable. Innovative approaches were taken, although, by and large, remote learning was not considered a tremendous success.

HOPE FOR THE FUTURE

The stories of students from Nepal are enlightening—and there are many similar stories all over the world. Young students anywhere can learn from online courses because they are so widely available. Local efforts by people like Mr. Baman Kumar Ghimire and Mr. Bishwa Raj Gautam to create a system of support are also essential to this success. In other words, we have students who are interested in learning outside their school. We have MOOCs and other online resources that have been created by various individuals and institutions. We also have adults who are able to create a local support system. These three elements are what we will need to cultivate different forms of learning in the future.

This book is about creating such a future. How do we do that? First, we must be able to imagine a bigger learning context for our students. For too long, students have been placed within the borders of learning. Their learning has been tightly linked to the *school pathway*, which specifies that all children need to be in school and go through schooling, grade by grade, before they can graduate and pursue higher learning or enter the workplace. The school pathway also gives students the borders of curriculum, assessment, and classroom: students' learning is limited to what has been prescribed in the curriculum, what is assessed, and what individual teachers teach in the classroom. However, given the recent advances in computer and mobile technology, students need not be so confined.

Second, we must encourage and enable students to take ownership of their own learning. One of the reasons that educational reforms have failed to deliver results is a lack of involvement by students. The reform efforts have been directed at strengthening the grammar of traditional schooling—enhancing the curriculum, strengthening teaching, and improving assessment. In other words, the goal was to strengthen the borders of learning. But students are the learners. They have their own passions and interests, strengths and weaknesses, and personal contexts. Unless they are involved as change makers and can make schooling work for them, it is unlikely that school outcomes will change. Moreover, to learn the new and emerging knowledge and skills required in the age of "smart" machines, students will have to follow different pedagogical approaches from traditional direct instruction. They will have to learn through experiencing, through inquiry, through working on projects, and through tackling unknown problems.

> Unless students are involved as change makers and can make schooling work for them, it is unlikely that school outcomes will change.

Third, local teachers and school leaders need to create an ecosystem to introduce students to and support their learning outside the school. The ecosystem should have the capacity to introduce students to opportunities and resources in the global ecosystem. It should also have personnel acting as advisors and facilitators to support the learning. In addition, it ought to involve small communities of learners and teachers working together to help each learner grow and participate in the global learning environment.

Finally, we need a lot of learning resources, institutions, mentors, experts, and educators around the world. These resources, institutions, and people, together with participating students, form the global ecosystem. This ecosystem is already there—with YouTube, Google, and all sorts of social media (as well as institutions and individuals) offering courses and learning experiences. This ecosystem can, of course, grow even further, and it is already doing so.

> The future of learning is students participating in a global learning ecosystem with the support of their local schools.

In this book, I present the future of learning, which is possible today. The future of learning is students participating in a global learning ecosystem with the support of their local schools. In this new ecosystem, students will be liberated from the borders of the previous, failed system.

There are many books and articles on how to improve schools and classrooms. There are also many arguments that schools are outdated and should be abolished. At this moment, neither approach has a chance of working well. It is doubtful that small improvements in the curriculum, in teaching, and in assessment can truly help our children develop the knowledge, skills, attitudes, and values required in the new world. At the same time, I don't believe that schools, as a social existence, can or should be abolished. What we need is to maintain schools as educational institutions but enact significant transformative changes. We need to create space and develop support for students to become the owners of their learning.

This book is a call to action. It is intended to help educators, education policy makers, parents, and students imagine a different kind of learning, a learning that is owned by students. This book has many examples of the forms and formats of the new learning, as well as examples of how to make such learning happen, but it is not my intention to present a step-by-step prescription for all educators and schools to make the change. I strongly believe that educators, school leaders, parents, and students are all capable of making significant and meaningful changes when they are sufficiently inspired and motivated. I also strongly believe that contexts matter—different classes and schools can and should make different changes. I want this book to inspire and motivate people to take action to make those big changes.

To make the big changes will require a lot of small changes in classrooms and schools. In Chapter 2, we will focus on the aspects of education that limit our students today. In Chapter 3, the discussion is about recent technological changes and the abundance of opportunities that now exist for students to learn outside of their school. Chapter 4 is about the school pathway, which has created borders within the school and which we should consider reorganizing. Chapter 5 discusses new possibilities to personalize the curriculum for all students. I propose that a student's curriculum can have three parts—government-mandated, school-mandated, and personal. In this way, students would have common knowledge and skills to help them function as citizens but also unique strengths and passions to enable them to thrive as individuals. Chapter 6 makes the argument for decentralized teaching and learning: Teachers no longer need to teach classes for all their students. They can arrange for students to learn in other ways, from outside sources of knowledge. This changes the teacher's role from traditional instructor to consultant and supporter. Chapter 7 turns to the learner. It discusses how to help each learner become self-determined and the owner of his or her learning. Chapter 8 brings it all together and discusses how we can help all students become *learners without borders*.

CHAPTER 2

The School Pathway

The public schools were designed like a roach motel. You are supposed to enter at age six and you can't leave until they stick a fork in you and proclaim that you are done.

(Russell, 2019)

This is Steve Russell's characterization of schools in his article "Schooling v. Education." Russell is enrolled Cherokee and went to school in Oklahoma. He dropped out at ninth grade but later earned a master's degree in judicial studies and became a judge, a writer, and an academic. His characterization of schools may be too harsh for some—particularly those who have been working very hard at making schools better—but his experiences of formal education during the 1950s were miserable and intolerable:

> I must also admit that I despised Bristow High School so much it made me crazy at times. Finding a place to hide where I could curl up with a book had been easy at Edison Elementary, but as I got to higher grade levels it became nearly impossible. It was as if I could not breathe within the building and I would start to hyperventilate half a block away to maximize how long I could hold my breath. (Russell, 2019)

Russell summarized the main cause of his experience this way: "The teachers lacked the authority to deviate from the approved curriculum and I lacked the inclination—some would say, the common courtesy—to apply myself to somebody else's priorities." Russell is a classic example of a student who did not fit into school's traditional borders.

Russell's reflection highlights the fundamental problem with the entire system of schooling. Russell's teachers could not deviate from the curriculum, which had been approved by some authority. In Russell's case, that authority would have been the Oklahoma State Department of Education or the local school district. Even if the teachers wanted to help Russell, to work with his passions and desires, they could not do much. They had to teach what the curriculum prescribed. The essence of the problems with schools is not teachers, school leaders, or policy makers. Everyone involved in schools wants to do good for students. However, schooling, as it has been conceived, consists of a series of well-designed borders that define what policy makers, school leaders, and teachers can actually do.

Teachers cannot deviate from the curriculum because the curriculum is made to serve all students and every student is required to master the curriculum. Technically, the curriculum is decided by a governing body and is subject to changes based on that body's reactions to societal changes and public opinions. Once changed, the curriculum applies to all teachers and students. In other words, whatever curriculum is being taught becomes one of the rules that govern schooling and must be applied to all students.

To look at it another way, the school could have a curriculum that fits Steve Russell very well but is unfit for some other students. Whether other students would have such a strong reaction as Russell did is hard to predict, but what is certain is that one curriculum does not work for all students. Some students may have the inclination to follow the curriculum anyway, but some may just decide to leave, as Russell did.

The curriculum is just one of the many limitations that cannot be deviated from in schools. In the 1990s, education historians David Tyack, Larry Cuban, and William Tobin (Tyack & Cuban, 1995; Tyack & Tobin, 1994) wrote about the "grammar of schooling": rules that dictate the operation of schools. These rules include age-based grouping, knowledge being splintered into school subjects, school time being fragmented into classes, an adult managing a group of students, and more. Only when these rules are implemented is a school an actual school in the eyes of the public.

These rules—which we'll cover in the chapters to come—are what I call *borders*. They define the space within which students learn. They specify what students can and cannot do with regard to their education. They also decide which students are "good" and which ones are "poor." In other words, when people become students in a school, they live within many borders. They cannot go beyond these borders, and their learning is sanctioned within these borders.

THE BORDERS OF SCHOOLING

Borders are inherent within schools. Think of them as the bricks that make up the school building. They are molded together and cannot be easily changed. Let us look at some of the most defining borders of schooling.

The Curriculum Border

Virtually all schools have a curriculum for their students that describes and defines the content that students can learn in a school. As explained earlier, the curriculum is often defined by a governing body at the national level, the state level, the school level, or a combination of the three. In the United Kingdom, Australia, and many other English-speaking countries, the curriculum is prescribed at the national level and applies to all students throughout the country. In the United States, on the other hand, curricula are derived from state standards and are decided at the district or school level.

Often splintered into different subjects and activities, a curriculum specifies what and when students should learn. It often also details how much time students should spend learning the various elements of the curriculum. Furthermore, it implies or specifies assessments—when students take what tests to demonstrate that they have learned what they are supposed to learn.

It seems natural that schools have a curriculum. A curriculum gives parents and the public a sense of what their children will learn and what we can expect these children will know and be able to do later. It tells school leaders and teachers what they should teach. And, most important, it defines what students should study when they are in school, whether or not it leaves room for students to learn what they may be interested in learning.

The curriculum is a powerful border for all students, for a number of reasons. First, it defines what it described as achievement. Students can learn anything—and they do, both within and outside school—but only that which is included in the curriculum and measured by related assessments is considered "real" and legitimate learning. Anything else, no matter how good, useful, or meaningful, is not measured and therefore is not considered part of a student's growth.

Second, a curriculum represents the voice and mind of the powerful—those who have the authority to decide the content that must be taught. This powerful group uses the curriculum to control what students are allowed to and must learn. Moreover, they are the ones who have become successful and control much of the social mechanisms to sort children into different roles. Students who are willing and able to complete the curriculum are rewarded; those who don't are typically left behind. As a result, very few students can openly reject the curriculum. If they do not like the curriculum, they may pretend to study it; when they can't manage that, they may just leave the school, as Russell did.

Third, mastering the curriculum consumes all the time students have in school and, in some places, outside school. While students may be allowed, or even encouraged, to have extracurricular activities, the majority of their life is dedicated to the curriculum. Because it is the school's responsibility to teach the curriculum, the entire school staff focuses on getting students to master it. As a result, as long as he or she is in school, a student can only have access to the learning available in the curriculum.

Fourth, there is only one curriculum for each core discipline area—or set of standards—in a school. Because the majority of the world's schools are public schools, operated by governments, most of them have the same curriculum—although the United States is an outlier in only prescribing a set of national standards. It is often the case that one curriculum serves millions of students. Even when curricula technically differ across state or national lines, what is in them is amazingly similar, with literacy and numeracy at the core, plus history, governments, sciences, foreign languages, and a few other alternatives. The result is that almost all students in the world study the same thing for nearly twelve years.

We'll discuss alternatives to the curriculum border in Chapter 5.

The Teacher Border

The teacher is another border that limits students in schools. A teacher is charged with responsibility for a group of students, which varies in size depending on how much the school costs and where the school is. Generally, in more expensive schools, a teacher is in charge of fewer students than in less expensive schools.

Their roles may vary slightly in different schools, but teachers are generally tasked with the same responsibility: teaching the students the subject(s) they are responsible for. Teachers are prepared in colleges of education to teach specific subjects. Every teacher must be able to teach at least one or perhaps two subjects in the curriculum. Their job is to make sure they teach the subjects while maintaining order in a well-managed classroom.

When in school, students are with a teacher virtually all the time. They are rarely given or have the opportunity to be on their own. While the curriculum determines what knowledge and skills students learn in the classroom, teachers determine how to teach the content and how each class "feels."

Teachers are presumed to be necessary for students, for a number of reasons. There is a general assumption that students cannot learn without being taught by a teacher. Furthermore, teachers must be around to ensure students are well-organized, so that they can learn. They are necessary to maintain order when students are together and make sure that students are behaving well toward each other. In other words, there is an underlying belief that students do not know how to learn and will behave poorly toward each other unless they are managed by teachers.

As a result—and, not surprisingly—students are subject to teachers. They rarely have the opportunity to pick their teachers. They must follow the teachers assigned to them and obey them completely. The student–teacher relationship largely favors the teacher, placing the teacher at a much higher level than the student. In essence, as soon as students are in school, they are dominated by teachers, who are also carriers of the powerful curriculum.

As a result, for as long as the students are in school, their learning is constrained and dominated by their teachers. They are within the borders of teachers, which we'll discuss further in Chapter 6.

The Classroom Border

The classroom is as old as schools; in fact, most schools started with just one room. Now each school is made up of many classrooms. Classrooms make another significant border that confines students. In schools, knowledge is splintered into subjects, and students of each subject are divided into classes, and each class is held within a classroom. A teacher teaches the class in the classroom. Unless the teacher makes an effort to bring in outside resources or take the class on a field trip, students are stuck in isolated physical classrooms. What they can have access to is limited to what is available in their classrooms.

The Age Border

Age is yet another border within which all students have to live in terms of learning. Schooling is first and foremost age-based. Children must reach a certain age in order to go to school, regardless of their physical, cognitive, psychological, and socio-emotional conditions. They then must spend a certain number of years in school before they can legally leave.

When children arrive at school, they are placed with a group of other children of or near the same age as them. And this group of children is asked to learn the same content and skills. Although some of them may already know the content and skills, and some others may be far behind, the assumption is that they all should know the same content and have the same skills by the end of the year, as assessed by the same tests.

Age is a big determinant in life, but it seems to play one of the most important roles for K–12 students. It places people in a spot—that is, school—where they have little freedom to follow their own passions and interest. On very few occasions can individuals break the border and study or do something else if they stay in school. We will look at rare examples of students who have done just that in Chapter 6.

The Graduation Border

Schools are divided into stages: primary (or elementary), middle, and high school. Although the division is sort of arbitrary, as suggested by the different number of years each stage occupies in different educational systems around the world, it is treated quite seriously in life. For example, students need to complete primary school before moving to middle school; they cannot simply decide when they are ready to go to middle school.

Moreover, in some places, moving from primary to middle school is not automatic but requires passing exams. Depending on the results of the exams, students can be sorted into different types of schools or different tracks. Likewise, in some systems, moving from middle school to high school requires examinations as well. The examination results can play a role in determining the type of high schools students can attend.

Schools operate on a readiness model: Each grade functions to get students ready for the next grade. Each level of schooling is meant to make students ready for the next level. In other words, students use their twelve or so years in school to become ready for what they will do next. When they reach the end of this period, they graduate and are presumed to be ready for college, careers, and life.

This graduation is another strong border of schooling. Before graduating, a person must stay in a school and spend his or her life on school-related matters. Only after graduation can he or she decide what to do with his or her life. Those who drop out of school, like Steve Russell, are typically considered "at risk," and opportunities are offered for them to study so they can make up the graduation by taking a high school equivalency test. In the United States, the GED (General Educational Development) is such a program.

The graduation border places students in school for a certain number of years. In most modern societies, the number of years is typically eleven to thirteen. During these years, students' primary job is to go to school and become ready for life after graduation. It is extremely difficult for students to do something other than attend school during this time. In most cases, it is against the law for children not to be in school. This border, together with other borders, seriously limits the opportunities that students can pursue in their own life.

THE DYSFUNCTIONAL ONE-TO-MANY MODEL

These borders make school a uniform experience for modern children. Everyone has to go to school and stay there for a certain number of years before they can do something else. The school follows the model of "one to many": one outcome for many students, one curriculum for many students, one pathway for many students, one teacher for many students, one assessment for many students, and one school for many students. Learning is bounded within the borders of standards, curricula, pacing guides, teachers, testing, classrooms, schools, and school districts. Learners thus pursue the same set of skills and knowledge, follow similar pathways, take the same tests, and learn from the same teachers within the same classroom defined by physical and virtual boundaries.

This one-to-many model was necessary for the Industrial Age. When our modern schools were constructed, the mass-production Industrial Age was beginning. The Industrial Age required a homogenous workforce with similar skills, so it was not surprising to see all students being taught the same skills and content. In addition, all school systems must also produce citizens, who require a certain level of common knowledge to function in the same society. It seems reasonable to expect all students to have similar knowledge.

Moreover, during the Industrial Age, teachers were the primary sources of knowledge. As a result, students had to go to a location where teachers were available. For efficiency's sake, each teacher had to teach a group of students. It is completely reasonable for teachers to be located in the place called "school" and for students to come to this place to learn. For over a hundred years, this one-to-many model of education has existed and matured. Despite the many problems and challenges they have faced, schools have prospered well.

However, this model is neither necessary nor functional anymore. The model has been criticized for a long time and for many reasons. It is beyond the scope of this book to list all the problems, although we will discuss the various borders identified. Instead, I highlight the most pressing and relevant issues.

Not Meeting the Needs of All Learners

One of the loudest criticisms of this model is that it does not meet the needs of all learners (Zhao, 2016, 2018c). The logic is simple: A one-size-fits-all model does not serve a tremendously diverse population of students who have different needs and purposes. The diversity of children, as due to the interactions between "nature" (genetics/heredity) and "nurture" (environment), is widely recognized (Ridley, 2003).

Children are born different from one another. They are physically different, with different genetic potentials for height, weight, and skin color. They have different talents and different cognitive strengths and weaknesses. They are different in temperament and personalities. They have different innate desires, interests, and passions.

The environments children are born into are different as well. Some children are born into families of musicians; others into families of mathematicians; still others into families that love sports and games. Some are born into families with abundance; others into families of poverty. Some are born into communities of resources; others into communities of desperation.

Different environments create different experiences for children. Their nature—that is, their natural instinct—interacts with their environment, and, together, these things make children who they are. A young boy with a gift for reading cannot know whether he is good at reading until he has a chance to interact with a book. A young girl will never realize her musical talent until shown a way of expressing and developing it. Likewise, only a child who is granted the opportunity to experience the beauty of math will go on to become a mathematical genius.

These different children come to school, to the one-size-fits-all school, at a certain age. Immediately, they are judged by the curriculum. The curriculum, especially in the age of accountability, highlights literacy and numeracy. Other subjects are there but have little significance. School leaders and teachers are much more concerned about how their students do on accountability assessments, which typically tests math and reading. As a result, children who come to school with good reading and math skills are welcomed and celebrated, because the curriculum favors them. Those who struggle with math and reading are considered "at risk" and given extra attention (if they are lucky) or paid no attention to. Either way, these children suffer.

There are many other ways school does not serve the students who don't naturally fit into the curricular expectations or the essential arrangements of schooling. In many classrooms, students are penalized for not showing up on time, for not sitting down or for sitting improperly, for not doing or turning in the homework as instructed, or for challenging the teacher. Students can also get in trouble for refusing to study the dictated content, for failing to comply with school rules, or for raising questions in class.

When students who may otherwise be talented find themselves incompatible with schooling, the majority of them are smart enough to choose to "pretend" to be in school. They pretend to study, to follow the teachers, to do the homework, and to take part in the exams. They exert little effort but manage to go through the years to graduate. Some others may play along in some but not all of their subjects, choosing what to study and what to ignore as much as they can. Then you have the dropouts, like Russell, who cannot stand school and have to leave. Of course, there are also students who learn to cope with the system. These students decide to accept the curriculum and the teacher as the ultimate source of approval. Success in school becomes so powerful for them that whether schooling ultimately fits their future or their needs becomes of no concern to them.

Not Meeting the Needs of the World

Another issue with the current model of education is that it fails to help children meet the challenges and needs of the world of today and tomorrow. While the term "21st century skills" suggests that students need a new set of skills and knowledge in the 21st century (Trilling & Fadel, 2009), schools are not yet equipping students with those skills. And we are already more than twenty years into the 21st century! In his 2008 book *The Global Achievement Gap: Why Even Our Best Schools Don't Teach the New Survival Skills Our Children Need—And What We Can Do About It*, Tony Wagner's assertion that even the best schools in the world are not preparing children for today and the future is certainly right on.

During the writing of this book, I interviewed several thought leaders in the field of education, and all of them agree with Wagner. I asked them all about their views on our current educational system. No one said it works well. Their reasons why the current model does not work do not vary much; in general, they have to do with not equipping students with the skills they need for today or for the future.

The ability to deal with uncertainty, for example, is a big issue for Ron Beghetto, a veteran researcher on creativity, a professor of education at Arizona State University, and the author of numerous articles and books, including *What If? Building Students' Problem-Solving Skills Through Complex Challenges* (2018b), *Beautiful Risks: Having the Courage to Teach and Learn Creatively* (2018a), and *Big Wins, Small Steps: How to Lead for and With Creativity* (2016). Ron believes that, whereas today's schools teach children to remember known answers to known problems, students need to come up with innovative solutions to uncertain problems. The world needs people who can react to uncertainties, which is the norm of the world today.

> My interview with Ron Beghetto is on my YouTube channel (Yong Zhao). To access all of the video interviews mentioned, type the following URL directly into your browser:
>
> http://bit.ly/ learnerswithoutborders

Ted Dintersmith, a businessman with experience in politics and education, shared similar views. Ted—who has become an influential education writer and filmmaker, with video and book products such as *Most Likely to Succeed* (Wagner & Dintersmith, 2016) and *What Schools Could Be* (Dintersmith, 2019)—said that he does not think schools are preparing students well for today, let alone tomorrow.

Milton Chen, founding director of the George Lucas Educational Foundation, which has focused on collecting evidence of educational innovations, and author of *Education Nation: Six Leading Edges of Innovation in Our Schools* (2010), holds a similar opinion. He does not believe that much more than 10 percent of American schools are actually doing any of the educational innovations and ideas that have come about over the past several decades. (Watch my discussions with Ted and Milton on my website, at http://bit.ly/learners withoutborders.)

Catlin Tucker, an innovative teacher who has also become an influential teacher trainer and author of multiple books, including *Balance With Blended Learning: Partner With Your Students to Reimagine Learning and Reclaim Your Life* (C. R. Tucker, 2020), said that the percentage of schools that actually enable teachers and students to shift their education into student-centered learning is very small. Most important, Catlin does not believe that schools serve children well.

Like Catlin, Julie Stern is a teacher who has transformed into an instructional coach to support school transformation. She is also an author of *Tools for Teaching Conceptual Understanding, Secondary: Designing Lessons and Assessments for Deep Learning* (Stern et al., 2017) and other books. Julie works with curricula but is deeply concerned that the way curricula are designed and implemented in schools can actually hurt education. (My interviews with Catlin and Julie can also be found at http://bit.ly/learners withoutborders.)

There is general agreement from these thought leaders and countless others that the traditionally valued skills and knowledge will become less important and a whole set of new capabilities will become more important (Barber et al., 2012; Florida, 2012; Pink, 2006; Wagner, 2008; Wagner & Dintersmith, 2016). While the specifics vary, the general agreement is that repetition, pattern prediction and recognition, memorization, and any skills connected to collecting, storing, and retrieving information are in decline because of AI and related technologies (Muro et al., 2019). On the rise is a set of skills that has many different names, such as "21st century skills," "soft skills," and "noncognitive abilities." These skills include creativity, curiosity, critical thinking, entrepreneurship, collaboration, communication, growth mindset, and a host of others (Duckworth & Yeager, 2015; Zhao, Wehmeyer, et al., 2019).

But the current model of education is not teaching students these skills. Moreover, we should be encouraging students' individuality, rather than praising conformity and homogeneity, so that students can thrive in the age of "smart" machines (Zhao, 2012, 2018c). Automation has already displaced millions of workers, and the Fourth Industrial Revolution will result in even more displacement. It is essential that the workers of the future (today's students) not compete with machines; instead, they need to develop their uniquely human abilities. Machines do not have (yet) our social and emotional qualities; therefore, according to Tim Cook, CEO of Apple, those qualities are of tremendous value to educators:

> [Teachers are] worried about machines taking jobs and AI sort of replacing humans. My worry is not that machines will think like people—it's that people will think like machines. And so that to me is a much bigger worry. (quoted in I. Fried, 2018)

And, of course, the one-size-fits-all education model is not helping students become more personalized, more unique, and more different from machines.

SUMMARY

Confining learners within the boundaries of a single pathway, a homogenous curriculum, a uniform set of standards and assessment, and a sole source of learning opportunities is damaging on a number of fronts.

First, it leads to tremendous waste of human potential because it does not provide opportunities, resources, and encouragement for developing the broad spectrum of natural human talents. Worse, it actively suppresses diversity by only valuing a narrow set of skills and knowledge in a limited number of domains.

Second, it leads to alienation and disengagement of a large proportion of children in the education process because they cannot find encouragement, support, or opportunities to learn what they are passionate about or interested in.

Third, it exacerbates the inequality in educational opportunities by limiting students to what's immediately available in their physical locations. As a result, children in disadvantaged communities suffer from poorer resources and teachers.

The current model of education may have been necessary at one time, but that necessity has diminished as technology has advanced. Our new society has made it possible to enjoy the full diversity of human potentials (Zhao, 2018d). Rising productivity has led to more leisure time and more disposable income, which enables human beings to consume more psychological, spiritual, intellectual, and psychological goods and services. These goods and services are personal and require a diversity of talents in their production. Further, it is also necessary now to cultivate a diverse workforce with different talents, passions, skills, and knowledge as machines replace the homogenous workforce with only mechanical skills. Finally, technology has made it possible for students to access a broad range of learning opportunities and resources beyond their immediate physical environments. Teachers are no longer the sole source of information for learners. We can now imagine a different model of education.

CHAPTER 3

New Learning Opportunities

When I began my schooling in China in 1972, the only electronic technology I had access to was a government propaganda loudspeaker. The loudspeaker, technically, was not intended for my learning; its purpose was to promote government policies and bring whatever the authorities considered needed to the villagers. But I was able to listen to its three daily broadcasts, each about one hour long.

The loudspeaker brought me into a world I had never experienced. My village is deep in the hills of southwestern China's Sichuan Province. There were no major roads to the outside world, just small paths. The village is about two miles from the township, but I don't remember visiting the township often. There was no particular reason for me to go there and, more important, the Chinese government regulated how frequently villagers could gather at the township, in order to curtail capitalist activities such as trading. Thus, my life was confined to my village and nearby villages.

The loudspeaker was one of hundreds scattered across the villages in the region. They were all wired to the central station in the Commune, which was located at the township. The Commune leadership decided what to broadcast, and it was always new and interesting to me. I heard about national meetings that took place in Beijing. I heard about national leaders passing and their memorial services. I also heard calls to prepare for wars with different imperialist nations such as the United States, which I had no idea about. Sometimes I heard songs and music, all communist revolutionary style.

The loudspeaker gave me a different and new world. Its content was far away from my village experience. The accent of the voices from the loudspeaker was different from that of my fellow villagers. The types of activities I heard were something I had never experienced and I could not imagine. I did not understand what was happening most of the time, but I was able to guess. Listening to the loudspeaker trained my imagination and creativity, allowing me to come up with my own interpretations of the broadcasts.

The loudspeaker technology was itself of great interest to me. I simply did not understand how it worked. I imagined that the wire was hollow, like bamboo, so that the voices could come through. We played games with bamboo, using a long bamboo stick, with the inside knots removed, to call each other. Once I actually picked up a downed loudspeaker wire and tried to see through it. It shocked me when I touched it, but I was able to look and see that it was not hollow.

My primary school was in another village, about one mile from my own. The school was just one room, with children of various ages. I had two teachers during primary school, one for first and second grades and the other for third to fifth grades. The school had literally nothing in terms of technological resources or a library. For most of my time there, we did not even have textbooks due to the Cultural Revolution, which turned China into a battlefield of political campaigns and economic turmoil. The teacher somehow managed to give us something to learn and something to do. So the loudspeaker was extremely significant for me. It piqued my curiosity and always inspired me to think beyond the context of my village.

Today, almost fifty years later, I have my iPhone and computer. I can access news from anywhere in the world. The news comes in videos and texts with very detailed images. I have over thirty thousand followers on Twitter, and they are scattered all over the world. I participate in Zoom meetings with audiences from every corner of the globe on a daily basis. I watch YouTube to learn all sorts of skills. I listen to podcasts created by people on different continents. I can talk to anyone from my home country using WeChat, for free. I have stayed home for more than eight months now because of the COVID-19 pandemic, but I feel very well connected with colleagues, collaborators, and my students at two universities in very distant locations—the University of Kansas in the United States and University of Melbourne in Australia.

THE IMPACT OF TECHNOLOGY

Over the past fifty years, technology has changed dramatically. It has transformed my life and the lives of millions. It has replaced hundreds of millions of jobs and led to the disappearance of millions more. It has, of course, created new jobs as well and led to the birth of new industries. It has created many winners, at the expense of rendering many others losers. It has enriched a small number of individuals and lifted a tremendous number out of poverty. It has also created an expanding income gap and vast inequalities. It has brought medical advances that save lives and increase lifespans, but it has caused massive damage to the environment. It has brought human societies closer than ever before but has fueled worldwide conflicts. It has shortened physical distances and collapsed national borders, but it has brought human beings into cultural, religious, and national battles.

All this is to say that the impact of technology is not easily determinable as good or bad. But it has been huge. It has affected literally everyone in the world, and the impact continues to expand. Technology will continue to alter human society for generations to come. Changes in the future will be faster and bigger. No one knows exactly how it may play out eventually, and everyone is a participant in the change, whether they wish to be or not. We experience changes made upon us, and we create changes to affect others.

Technology has affected schools as well—but the impact has been relatively small. By and large, the fundamentals of schools remain. The basic "grammar of schooling" (Tyack & Cuban, 1995; Tyack & Tobin, 1994) today is the same as it was fifty or even a hundred years ago. Knowledge is still splintered into subjects or discipline areas. Subjects are still taught in class periods. The school time is still divided into class periods of forty-five or fifty minutes. Students are still grouped based on age, and each group of students forms a class, which is still taught and managed usually by one adult—the teacher. How students are taught remains relatively the same, as well.

What students are taught may have been updated a bit to reflect the changes in the world, but the overall curriculum largely remains similar to that of fifty years ago. Students are still assessed at the end of each course, and large, standardized tests judge what is considered important: reading, math, and science.

There are many reasons for the lack of big changes in schools. Larry Cuban, former education historian at Stanford University, has proposed that when technology meets teachers, teachers win, which means that teachers remain unchanged by technology (Cuban, 1986, 1993). So far, it looks as if Cuban was right. But will Cuban be right in the future? About ten years ago, Harvard business professor Clayton Christensen and colleagues' book *Disrupting Class, Expanded Edition: How Disruptive Innovation Will Change the Way the World Learns* (2010), with its core prediction that education would be drastically changed by virtual learning, gained much popularity among educators. While Christensen's prediction is far from being realized today, was he largely wrong or will he be proven right someday soon?

The COVID-19 pandemic helped Christensen's argument a little bit, although he passed away in January 2020 and thus was unable to see it for himself. The coronavirus indeed increased the number of schools using remote learning. But this change was not a result of convincing and converting teachers. Nor was it a result of students choosing online learning. Instead, the increase was a result of something that had nothing to do with education. The change was not voluntary and will not likely last very long. As soon as schools resume normal operation, it is very possible that COVID-induced online learning will be abandoned.

Whether technology has had a significant impact on education is perhaps irrelevant to the future because education has to change and because technology plays a significant role both as a major reason for the changes and as a tool that can facilitate the changes.

First, technology's impact on societies and the economy has already put pressure on education to produce high-school graduates with talents, skills, knowledge, and attributes different from those of past graduates. Second, technology has already created a different atmosphere for education to operate in. And, third, technology has had tremendous impact on the students in schools.

WHAT MATTERS: THE PRESSURE ON EDUCATION

In *The Race Between Education and Technology*, Harvard economists Claudia Goldin and Lawrence Katz (2008) observed a very interesting relationship between education and technology. The relationship is fairly straightforward. Technology causes changes in society, dismantling some industries and giving birth to new industries, thus raising the value of some skills and decreasing the value of others. In order for the masses to catch up, to take advantage of the new technologies instead of being disadvantaged by technological advances, we need to upgrade education to teach the skills that have increased value. If education can win the race and help the masses develop the needed skills, prosperity will be shared. If not, the technological innovators will do well, but the masses won't. The result will be massive unemployment and under-employment, widening income inequality, and social turmoil.

America and many other developed countries have already seen widening income gaps and the disappearance of the middle class. We are already in the process of social turmoil. There is rising xenophobia, there are increasing racial and religious conflicts, and political isolationism is trending. While there are many reasons for the social unrest around the world, it is not unreasonable to make education's failure in the race with technology a major reason.

Technological changes over the past few decades have created a different society. America is not the same as it was in the 1960s or 1970s. Automation has replaced millions of jobs. Technology has resulted in another wave of globalization, which enabled millions more jobs to be outsourced to cheap workers in poorer nations. Schools should have responded by teaching students new skills, but they have not. Instead, government policies have driven schools to focus on the most basic education outcomes: closing the test-score gaps in reading and math. Reading and math are, of course, important, but the way schools have been forced to improve reading and math has been very problematic and unlikely to yield results (Zhao, 2018e). And the achievement gap, which in essence is defined as test-score gaps, *cannot* be closed, because of societal, historical, psychological, and cultural reasons. Moreover, the gaps are not necessarily that meaningful or important when examined from different perspectives, because they can be either compensated for with strengths in other areas or removed at a later stage if children are given the opportunity to develop their strengths and interests (Zhao, 2016).

In Chapter 2, we discussed the need for "21st century skills," which include creativity, entrepreneurial abilities, curiosity, critical thinking, collaboration, resilience, communication, global competence, financial competence, digital competence, and a host of other skills. Besides these skills, technology also gives rise to the "useless" talents, skills, and knowledge that have been traditionally viewed as of less value (Zhao, 2012, 2018d).

As I wrote in "The Rise of the Useless" (2018d), technology has fundamentally changed the consumption of talents and skills. We used to consume similar skills and talents a hundred years ago, but as technology has increased our productivity, it has given us two important things—more leisure time and increased income. More leisure time means that people work much less than before, and now they need to seek activities during the increased time of leisure. More income means that people in developed countries have drastically increased their income beyond what is needed for simple survival, so they can spend more money on nonessential activities. Thus, in the modern era there is an increased need for arts, music, entertainment, services, tourism, health, fashion, and other things that make us feel good psychologically. Recent growth in these areas requires new skills and talents. Many of the talents that could help people thrive in these areas have not been deliberately cultivated in schools.

The pressure that technology places on education continues. Artificial intelligence (AI), big data, the Internet of Things (IoT), nanotechnology, and all sorts of new technological advancements have not stopped. Instead, they are accelerating. Driverless automobiles are likely to replace millions of truck drivers, bus drivers, and of course taxi and ride-share drivers. Online payment systems have already displaced and will continue to displace millions of bank tellers.

The possible near-future impact of AI was interestingly framed in a Brookings Institution study (Muro et al., 2019) in which researchers analyzed descriptions of the functions of AI-related patents and compared these to descriptions of people's job functions in labor statistics. Based on similarities between words and phrases in these two textual realms, they concluded that better-paid, better-educated workers face the most exposure to the spread of AI. In other words, AI is most likely to displace college graduates who hold high-paying jobs, because the description of the tasks that AI can do mostly closely matches theirs.

This is a serious warning. Whereas previous automation has displaced workers with lower education from mostly jobs that require manual labor (e.g., factory work), AI and associated technologies are about to enter the world of educated and highly compensated people. They are breaking into the cognitive and knowledge world. This change is already under way and is happening fast. A 2020 jobs report claimed that, in about five years, "the time spent on current tasks at work by humans and machines will be equal" (World Economic Forum, 2020, p. 5). The report urgently highlights the continuation of the skills gap:

> The top skills and skill groups which employers see as rising in prominence in the lead up to 2025 include groups such as critical thinking and analysis as well as problem-solving, and skills in self-management such as active learning, resilience, stress tolerance and flexibility. On average, companies estimate that around 40% of workers will require reskilling of six months or less and 94% of business leaders report that they expect employees to pick up new skills on the job, a sharp [uptick] from 65% in 2018. (World Economic Forum, 2020, p. 5)

Further, the report says that the "future of work has already arrived for a large majority of the online white-collar workforce" and the majority of employers are expected to expand remote work. About 44 percent of the employers' work is expected to operate remotely.

The only way in which education can respond to these drastic changes is for it to urgently catch up with technology. Education must take the challenges brought about by technology seriously. Rather than continuing to struggle for the so-called excellence measured by traditional tests in math and reading, education has to take on helping students acquire the new skills and develop the new mindset they will need in the world of tomorrow.

NEW STUDENTS AND THEIR INTERACTIONS WITH TECHNOLOGY

The students of today were born in the age of "smart" devices and an interconnected world. The youngest, the ones who are entering school now (in 2021), were born in 2015 or 2016 and will graduate around 2033. This group of students has had a very different life from those in the 1960s or 1970s. Today's youths live in a digital world, one that did not exist in their grandparents' or even their parents' time.

The digital world has been in the making for a long time (Negroponte, 1995; Tapscott, 1998; Turkle, 1995; Zhao, 2009). The arrival of "smart" devices, such as smartphones, has made it ubiquitous. For most adults, participation in the digital world is unavoidable. Work, entertainment, education, shopping, and socializing can all be done digitally. In fact, adults who are not able to use technology are disadvantaged in some circumstances.

Youths also live in the digital world. In fact, they perhaps spend more time on technology than many adults. A study shows that today's youths in the United States spend more time on screen media than in school. A 2019 survey by the Common Sense Media Census found that eight-to-twelve-year-olds spent about five hours (four hours and forty-four minutes) per day on screen media. Teens spent almost seven and a half hours, not including using technology for school-related work (Rideout & Robb, 2019). In the United States, students generally spend five to six hours in school per day, and a typical school year is 180 days. This means that the average student spends about twice time as much on screen media as he or she spends in school in a year.

Spending so much time on screen media means that students have great access to an outside world beyond their immediate environments. The government propaganda loudspeaker of my childhood gave me an idea of a world beyond my village, but it was very limited and tightly controlled by the broadcaster. Today, students have unlimited access to the outside world, literally anywhere in the world, via YouTube, TikTok, Instagram, Facebook, Twitter, and an ever-increasing list of applications on their phones and computers. The content is created by users all over the world, in both urban and remote areas, and is more diverse than anyone could have imagined fifty years ago. It can be good or bad, virtuous or damaging.

Not only do today's students have access to the outside world, but also they can interact with the outside world, unlike me when I was their age. They can exchange comments on YouTube or other platforms. They can directly interact with their "friends" on Facebook. They can post and share information on Twitter. They can publish their own content in video, audio, text, cartoon, or other formats, which others can consume and comment on.

Moreover, today's youths can have control over their access to and interactions with the outside world. They can choose what they view, listen to, and read. They can also have control over with whom they interact. They can decide what to do with the comments they receive and what comments they want to share. They can decide how long to maintain the interactions they want to be engaged with. Overall, youths today have the possibility of having control of the outside world they interact with.

Today's youths can live a life separate from school and family. They can live online. They can shop online, play video games online and with players from around the world, create content and post it online, learn online by viewing content created by others and interacting with others, and work online as well. This online world is definitely different from the world I had access to via the loudspeaker or the world that other people had access to via radio, TV, and newspapers. For many youths it is a third world, aside from their school world and their family world.

We, as adults, may prohibit our children from accessing social media and online environments. Quite a lot of parents do not give their children access to these things—but a lot of parents have. Eventually, most parents give in and grant their children access when they reach a certain age. Many students, by the time they are twelve, have access to this amazing online world in various ways.

The power and influence of social media cannot be overestimated. On the positive side, the world the government propaganda loudspeaker gave me fifty years ago inspired me and kept me imagining a life outside of my village. It was a powerful experience that drove me beyond what I was born into. I think it is no exaggeration to say that the same can happen for many youths today, especially those who are economically disadvantaged.

Of course, on the negative side, social media can be dangerous. It has led to cyberbullying. It has fueled video-game addictions. It has allowed unfortunate youths to become entangled in unhealthy online relationships. Furthermore, it has circulated misinformation and conspiracy traps that have had serious effects.

The outside world today's youths interact with can be extremely valuable. It can also be a total loss of time or even dangerous. We should not underestimate or ignore its power. It would be a mistake to shut our children away from it—it is too pervasive and cannot be truly irrelevant to our children. What we, as parents and educators, should do is appreciate the value of this world and guide our children to interact well with it (Zhao, 2020b).

It is important that educators consider the fact that today's children have access to and interact with the external world. This world has a lot more information and people than any school can offer. Youths today know a lot more things and can be interested in many more activities than we'd like to imagine. They may be more connected, more sophisticated, and more capable than they are typically thought to be. We cannot view today's youths as simply having a school life and a family life. What they physically do is just a small piece of their real life.

HOW TO IMPROVE: THE OPPORTUNITIES

In the 1990s, the dream was to connect classrooms to the Internet, or the "information superhighway." The ideal situation was for every five students to have access to an Internet-connected computer. Today, most schools in developed countries are way beyond that ideal. Ironically, ease of access to the internet has become a problem for many schools. Students' "smart" devices, such as phones that can connect to the Internet, are banned in some schools. Teachers do not want to be disrupted or distracted by students' virtually ubiquitous access to the Internet all the time.

The drive to connect students to the Internet in the 1990s and early 2000s was meant to ensure that students had access to the emerging information superhighway so that their learning could take place beyond the classroom. The assumption was that students could form learning communities with people in other schools and other contexts. They could learn from people, institutions, and materials in faraway places. They could go on virtual tours of museums. They could participate in scientific experiments conducted in remote national labs. They could travel to outer space and deep oceans virtually with scientific equipment.

Today, hardware and software connectivity is much better than we imagined. The power of technology to support educational activities has, in many ways, exceeded our hopes of thirty years ago, let alone fifty years ago. Students can actually do what was dreamed. Here is a brief summary of the benefits that technology presents for educational purposes.

Broad Access to Information

Students can instantly find not only books and articles written in the recent and distant past, but also information in the making. Google has digitized millions of books, and various services provide instant access to published scientific journals, magazines, and humanities databases. There is also instant access to music, movies, TV shows, and other audio and video products. Additionally, almost all museums have extensive websites and provide virtual access to their holdings.

Learning Apps

As of the writing of this book, there are over 2.2 million apps on the Apple App Store and over 2.8 million on the Google Play Store. While not all the apps are educational, the ones that are educational cover a wide range of topics and subjects, from early reading to advanced science. These apps also take different approaches to learning, from playful multimedia games to traditional, serious lecture-style presentations. Some are specifically meant to prepare people to take certain exams; others are general exploratory journeys. There are, of course, "good" apps that help people learn and "bad" apps that are a simple waste of time. What is important is the breadth and diversity of learning apps. Students can choose the ones that are of value and discard those that are no good. It is also important to point out that the number of apps is growing fast, with new ones being published all the time.

Online Courses/MOOCs/Khan Academy

Online courses designed to teach school subjects are numerous and diverse as well. There are many online courses designed by K–12 schools. There are also many massively open online courses (MOOCs) offered by universities and individuals. Khan Academy is one of the best-known online educational institutions, but there are many like it. There are individual teacher-made courses and also courses created by other experts. These courses may not all be applicable to all students, but there is no need to have one course fitting all students. The diversity of students' needs is best supported by the diversity in online courses, MOOCs, and modules provided on Khan Academy and other platforms. Their growth and diversity are precisely what schools and students need because they enable students to make choices.

YouTube

I highlight YouTube here because of its uniqueness. The website was launched in 2005 and has grown to be the second most popular site in the world. With over 130 million users, YouTube gets over 30 million visitors per day and 2 billion active users per month. Every minute, more than 300 hours of video are uploaded to YouTube, and 5 billion videos are watched every single day on YouTube. (Omnicore Agency, 2020)

More important, the site hosts countless learning materials from all over the world, most of which are free. One can learn how to cook, how to fix a refrigerator, how to swim, how to solve math problems, how to interact with people, or how to play guitar. There is content beyond one's imagination.

Social Media

Social media are another major resource for schools. With 2.7 billion Facebook users, 800 million TikTok users, 705 million LinkedIn users, 112.5 million Instagram users, and 330 million Twitter users (Statista, 2021a, 2021b), social media platforms are widely available and have been used broadly. Social media are not only tools for people to stay in touch, to share stories of their lives, or to spread news, but also tools for people to organize learning activities, to form learning communities, and to make connections with people anywhere. There are, again, "bad" uses of social media, but there are plenty of "good" uses. Social media are of tremendous potential for developing global learning environments and for engaging students in learning activities that span national and cultural boundaries.

Intelligent Tutoring Systems

Intelligent tutoring systems (ITS) have a long history in education (Sleeman & Brown, 1982). ITS are computer programs that personalize instruction for students by modeling students' knowledge and psychological states. They collect data about how students approach problems, which tells them about when they are likely to be motivated and when they are likely to be frustrated. The system improves the lessons and assessments by evolving in response to the learner. According to an article in *Education Week*,

> Intelligent-tutoring systems like ALEKS (for Assessment and LEarning in Knowledge Spaces), Cognitive Tutor, and a new program in development by IBM's Watson initiative are starting to expand in K-12 education, and experts argue that teachers need new training not only to use intelligent systems in the classroom but also to prepare students for careers in increasingly technology-integrated fields. (Sparks, 2017)

Over the years, with the advancement of AI, ITS have become much more sophisticated.

Large-Scale Learning Environments

Large-scale learning environments are online learning environments that involve a massive number of users, such as Minecraft, Scratch, and fanfiction websites. Learning, in these environments, is largely community-based and voluntary. Participants are very interested in the topic and activities. They provide each other with support and peer tutoring (Aragon & Davis, 2019; Dezuanni, 2020). Although not much of the learning is considered valid or even considered in schools, these environments can be powerful tools for teachers and schools to consider.

Live Communication Tools

Today we have access to an abundant set of live communication tools. Social media allow instant texting and sharing of videos and graphics. Google Hangouts, Microsoft Teams, Zoom, and a lot of other synchronous tools enable instant meetings with hundreds or thousands of people from around the world. These tools allow individuals to have access to experts and participate in meetings. These meetings can be saved, archived, and broadcast on social media and websites.

These are just a few of the many examples of tools that schools and teachers might use. They have tremendous potential for learning in different ways, ways that can help students meet the challenges laid out by technology. But these tools cannot replace teachers. Instead, they push teachers to take very different roles than in traditional instruction.

SUMMARY

In the past fifty years, technology has transformed our lives. The world is much more connected than ever before. Even people in my village now have access to the Internet and smartphones. I can call or video-chat with them at any time. I can text them at any time. This reality was unimaginable just a few years ago.

However, ironically, the children in my village are going to the same school I used to go to. I don't mean the same school physically; I'm referring to the *content* of the school. They don't have access to the external world when they are in school. They don't interact with people outside their school. They still listen to the teacher, study the textbook, and do the homework. They have a new world they must face, but they are studying the same content as we did fifty years ago, albeit they now have textbooks.

COVID-19 has changed the world. Although we don't know the whole picture of the impact of the coronavirus, we have a sense of its impact on education after almost a year. Schools will face budget cuts. Less money will be available to support schools as before. Schools will have to spend money on keeping students and staff healthy and safe. School leaders will have to think about the different world students will live in. We know that COVID-19 has gotten parents to interact with schools more. We also know that students and staff have gone through very unexpected and challenging times, which may have affected their psychological well-being. Lastly, we know that almost all students and teachers have gone through a period of learning differently, with remote learning.

Much has been written about the loss of learning during the pandemic and the difficulties of remote learning (Barnum, 2020; Shafer, 2020). The concerns over learning loss due to school closures are justified; not every student had the same level of access to technology, to remote learning, and to the same quality of instruction.

The learning loss may be real, but it may only have to do with what is in the curriculum. Students, given their different circumstances, may not have been able to learn what teachers are supposed to teach them in schools (i.e., what is prescribed in the curriculum). But, with the right mindset and education, gains may also have been made. Schools may have worked with students and parents to help students develop resilience and adaptability. During challenging and uncertain times, resilience and adaptability are what is needed to thrive.

As we move forward and try to apply what we have learned from the crisis, it is time to help students develop a sense of creativity and entrepreneurial thinking, so that they can be innovative and take charge of their own learning. Because many of them will continue to lack the constant supervision they once had in school, students will have to learn differently, with much more independence, self-regulation, and self-determination (Wehmeyer & Zhao, 2020).

These possibilities can be better realized if students have more freedom and more space in their own learning. We need a transformation in which students are encouraged to learn beyond the immediate instruction in the classroom and school, in which teachers care more about the child than the content, and in which learning can take place anywhere and anytime. This requires us to expand our idea of learning beyond the school, the curriculum, and instruction. The borders of schooling have constrained students for too long. To better prepare our children, schools need to take advantage of the technological tools available to create a better educational journey for all children.

CHAPTER 4

Changing the School Pathway

In 2008, at the age of ten, Noa Mintz started her first business: She ran art classes for kids during the summer, for a small fee. According to a *Forbes* magazine report (Marinova, 2016), at the age of twelve, Noa founded a children's party–planning business. By 2016, the eighteen-year-old entrepreneur operated a full-service childcare agency in New York City called Nannies by Noa, which matches nannies with families in need of a caregiver. While still in high school, she had hired a full-time CEO and a staff to run her business.

The *Forbes* report, with the title "18 Under 18: Meet the Young Innovators Who Are Changing the World," is a list of eighteen teenage entrepreneurs—that is, children who are still in school but are working on businesses that may change the world.

It may be difficult to know how many teenage entrepreneurs there are out there today. But in the United States, a survey by global youth organization Junior Achievement and accounting giant Ernst & Young found that 41 percent of teens would consider entrepreneurship as a career option instead of working in a traditional job. Already, about 6 percent of teen boys and 4 percent of teen girls had started a business (Junior Achievement of Greater Washington, 2018). In the United Kingdom, a study found that, between 2009 and 2018, the number of teenagers running their own businesses jumped from 491 to 4,152, an increase of 700% (BBC News, 2019).

It is important to point out that these teens have started their businesses largely on their own instead of as a result of the education they receive in school. It is also worth noting that the percentage of teen business owners is going up, largely as a result of new technologies that have made it easier for individuals to start and operate their own businesses (BBC News, 2019). Such new technologies and the COVID-19 pandemic are likely to bring more teens into entrepreneurship in the future.

A significant challenge for these teenage entrepreneurs is that they are still in school and they must graduate. They live within the borders of schooling, in particular the borders of age-determination and graduation. Trapped within these borders, these children have to take courses they may not be interested in. They must complete homework that may have nothing to do with their businesses.

Juggling business and school is not easy, as reported in a special program by Australia's 7 News (Cullen, 2019). The program, which followed the lives of several millionaire teenage entrepreneurs, received more than 2.5 million views on YouTube between August 2019 and July 2020. For Jack Bloomfield, one of the entrepreneurs featured, "the biggest challenge is carefully balancing being an entrepreneur with finishing Year 12" (Cullen, 2019). Jack was quoted as telling the reporter: "It's an uphill battle trying to fit in school, business, homework, sport—all that other stuff—and try and be a normal seventeen-year-old at the same time" (Cullen, 2019). The problem is the same for other teenage entrepreneurs in the film. Ali Kitinas, for instance, found being an entrepreneur and going to school more challenging than she had imagined. But she was hopeful:

> I try to balance as best as I can. This year has been a little bit tough. I was very aware that this year's business would take a bit of a back seat because it is my final year. [But] I can continue once I am in the real world and it becomes my full-time job, working for myself. (quoted in Cullen, 2019)

THE SCHOOL PATHWAY

Ali Kitinas has to put her business on the back burner because she has to go to school and finish school. So do many other teenage entrepreneurs. Can they not go to school and just focus on their businesses? Do they have to go and finish school? It's a relevant question—not just for the small (but increasing) number of teenage entrepreneurs, but for all students who don't see themselves following the traditional school pathway.

The answer is probably not. First, there is the issue of perception and mindset. Schools have existed for a long time, particularly in developed countries. They have become an integrated part of the culture. Children are supposed to go to school at a certain age and be there for a certain number of years before they can leave. Finishing school is what is expected of all children, and attending school is the children's primary job. In fact, very few people question whether they should send their children to school. They just do it when their child reaches a certain age, with great joy and high hopes.

The second issue is legality. Globally speaking, most countries have laws that require all children to be in school for a certain period of time. The compulsory education laws in many countries mandate parents, with few exemptions, to send their children to school or offer a similar type of education for their children. There are also other laws or legal requirements for children to be freed from child labor. These laws have been extremely valuable for societies to provide an opportunity for all children to have a similar educational experience, to build a workforce and citizenry, to offer all children a pathway toward social mobility, and to save children from hazardous child labor.

Third, school serves as a convenient childcare facility for many parents who need to work away from home. They would like their children to stay in school as long as possible. The COVID-19 pandemic has made this very visible. When schools are closed and children are home, it causes tremendous inconvenience and adds to the burden of many parents who still have to work, even at home. For many parents and families, their economic stability depends on having this option available for their children.

Moreover, school plays a significant, if not the only, role in an individual's social mobility in many societies, especially in developed countries. The school pathway is typically the proven and widely accepted way for individuals to progress in life, opportunity, and prosperity. Without finishing school, there is little possibility for individuals to achieve success. Typically, in more developed economies, the number of years one spent in school is highly associated with one's personal income. That is, the more years of schooling one has, the more money he or she usually earns as an adult.

School has gradually evolved into an essential element of society. It has become one of the unshakable pathways for human life: Children go to school at a certain age; they graduate from elementary school and then move on to middle school, and then to high school. After high school, some people go on to college or other postsecondary institutions for further training. After college, there are master's and doctoral programs, if one wishes to continue. This pathway, although with variations in different societies, is generally accepted around the world.

RETHINKING THE SCHOOL PATHWAY

Teenage entrepreneurs present us with an excellent opportunity to rethink the school pathway; they are compelled to follow this well-accepted pathway in society and, yet, still find ways to do much more than the pathway allows. The pathway expects and demands that all students finish a certain number of years of schooling before they can do something else. It does not enable or support children to pursue objectives outside its prescription.

But things have begun to change—in particular, as the internet has become faster and more accessible. Children suddenly have more options to engage in real economic activities. Before the internet, real work that is of economic value typically took place outside the home, in the workplace: factories, offices, and shopping centers. It was difficult, and actually illegal, for these places to hire children to do work. Hence, other than in a few exempted professions, such as acting and entertainment, children could not have access to regular work for economic purposes.

But since the early 1990s, the Internet and associated technological advancements have transformed how we work and live. What was impossible to imagine has become reality. From eBay to Amazon, from Google to Apple iPhones, from YouTube to Facebook, from Airbnb to TikTok, and from FedEx to UPS, technology has created the possibility for people to reach an audience in the billions and deliver goods around the globe. Being able to reach billions makes it possible for anyone to market their talents, skills, and goods globally. This includes children.

As a result, there has been a dramatic increase in the number of children engaged in economic activities. Young children profit from posting videos on YouTube and other platforms. Others profit from allowing people to watch them play video games online. There are children who make foods or other products and market these on the internet. There is also money to be made by writing product reviews.

In many ways, the internet, together with other technologies and services, has made it possible for children to fully participate in many economic activities in the world. They can run their own businesses. They can help with family businesses. They can and also do join hands with others to operate enterprises. They can also be freelance workers for companies.

It is important to point out that much of the work children do for economic value does not involve heavy labor or difficult conditions. More important, at least in the case of teenage entrepreneurs, children are engaged in these economic activities voluntarily instead of forced into them. Their work is not child labor as defined by relevant legislation.

But schools have not changed. Students are trapped within the borders of the school pathway, struggling to balance their entrepreneurial work and school. Very often these entrepreneurs have to sacrifice their businesses in order to attend school, because of the power of the school pathway.

BREAKING OUT OF THE SCHOOL PATHWAY

Greta Thunberg is another type of teenage entrepreneur: a social entrepreneur. She did not start a business; she started a global movement by skipping school. In August 2018, when she was fifteen years old, Thunberg began protesting outside the Swedish parliament. She stood alone, holding a sign that read *Skolstrejk för klimatet* ("School Strike for Climate"). Then another person joined her, then more, then hundreds, then thousands, and finally millions all over the world. Because of her achievement, in 2019 she was named *Time* magazine's Person of the Year. According to the *Time* story,

> In the 16 months since [beginning her activism], [Thunberg] has addressed heads of state at the U.N., met with the Pope, sparred with the President of the United States and inspired 4 million people to join the global climate strike on September 20, 2019, in what was the largest climate demonstration in human history. Her image has been celebrated in murals and Halloween costumes, and her name has been attached to everything from bike shares to beetles. Margaret Atwood compared her to Joan of Arc. After noticing a hundredfold increase in its usage, lexicographers at Collins Dictionary named Thunberg's pioneering idea, *climate strike,* the word of the year. (Alter et al., 2020)

Thunberg became a global symbol, with millions of followers around the world. Whatever her eventual impact may be, she has done more than any other person so far to address the issue of climate change. In less than two years, she successfully created a global movement calling for urgent changes. She not only provided a clear moral call to those who are willing to change, but also placed shame on those who are not. She has convinced political leaders to make policies and pass laws to eliminate the carbon footprint. She has inspired hundreds of youths to be like her—skipping school to lead in climate strikes all over the world (Alter et al., 2020).

Thunberg's rise was enabled by technological tools that were unavailable twenty years ago. Social media were key to her success. Twitter, Facebook, Instagram, and WhatsApp helped her reach a global audience in a matter of minutes. When news of her actions reached them, some people resonated with the message and took their own actions to start climate strikes. This is significant because when a person has an idea, the idea may not resonate with many people in a local community. This was the case for Thunberg. Although her teachers and her fellow students may have sympathized with her, they did not support her skipping school to strike. They did not join her, but the message reached out to people beyond her immediate community, and some people, a small percentage, participated. The size of the global audience is in the billions. A small percentage of a very large population can be a lot of people, enough not to be ignored.

Social media tools and other Internet-enabled technologies have already created a different generation of youths. The members of Generation Z and now Generation Alpha (Pinsker, 2020) grew up in a time when digital technologies were already generally available. They were born after the Internet revolution of the early 1990s. When the first among them reached adulthood, social media tools and "smart" devices were already in the making and quickly became accessible. Today's teens spend more time on media than they do in school (Rideout & Robb, 2019; Zhao, 2020b). This means that youths today are much more connected to the outside world, much more influenced by the broad world, and more likely to take actions to influence the broad world than previous generations were.

DROPPING OUT OF THE SCHOOL PATHWAY

Young entrepreneurs struggle to balance business and school, but they are often fortunate to be able to somehow manage the school pathway anyway. There is another group of students who struggle with school but, unlike the business-minded teens, are unable to find peace with it. These are the ones who decide to drop out.

This group comprises a much larger number of youths. These students may be passionate about and insistent on learning and doing something that the school offers little or no support of. Think about the dancers, the musicians, the artists, the designers, the game developers, or the writers. Aside from peripheral courses or clubs, students who have talents and are passionate about almost any area outside the core subjects have little opportunity in school to develop these talents. These students either have to purchase learning opportunities outside school, if their families have the resources, or simply let go of their talent and passions. Moreover, these students may or may not have a strong interest in learning the school subjects. And if not, they are the ones most likely to leave school.

The school pathway offers only one set of predetermined experiences for all children and uses predetermined exams to judge students. Many students find it difficult to follow. They may have other talents and passions they would like to pursue, but they are stuck in the school pathway and must comply. They gradually become disengaged with schooling. They may continue to stay in school but not pay attention to what happens. And when the time comes, they graduate and leave. Some others may decide to drop out without finishing, as early as possible, in order to pursue something else, although it may not be productive for them and society.

School dropouts in the United States number in the millions (APA, 2012). It is very difficult to simply attribute the decision to drop out to the inability of these students. These students may well be great in certain areas of academics but against the prescription of schooling. They are in many ways defeated by the school and then have to stay in it.

CHANGING THE SCHOOL PATHWAY

It seems apparent that the school pathway is not for everyone, but it has continued for a long time without much change (Tyack & Cuban, 1995; Tyack & Tobin, 1994). Students who struggle seem to have no option but to keep struggling or leave. However, the school pathway can be changed. Schools are human-made institutions, and the school pathway is as well. Our predecessors created these institutions to fit the needs of their society. Now that they no longer serve our students, it is time to change the system. In order to make this change, we must overcome two mindsets.

The Preparation Mindset

The Preparation Mindset dominates the thinking of parents, students, and most educators. This mindset believes that schooling is preparation for a successful life after school. The Preparation Mindset puts students, parents, and teachers at ease with the school pathway, making it very clear that the years one spends in school are in aid of something else in the future. It also makes it clear that each year of schooling is just groundwork for the next year. And then suddenly, when the time comes, students graduate as capable future workers.

Educational systems and governments are the creators of the school pathway, so they are the ones that developed the Preparation Mindset. They made the age-based grouping a common practice in many schools, through grade-level-based curriculum and assessment. They also created different stages of schooling—elementary, middle, and high school.

To change the school pathway, we must change the Preparation Mindset because it limits what students and schools can do. First, education is life, as John Dewey wrote over one hundred years ago: "I believe that education is a process of living and not a preparation for future living" (Dewey, 1897, p. 78). The time children spend in school is long, about ten to twelve years. This time is also one of the most important periods of life for a child developmentally. During this time, children grow in various domains—physically, socially, emotionally, and cognitively—through interactions with their environment. School is one of the environments they spend the most time in, and it is supposed to be the place dedicated to their growth and learning. Thus, school should be a place that supports children's natural development instead of just teaching them to become useful for the future (Grobstein & Lesnick, 2011). In addition, the twelve years that children spend in school actually matters as part of their life, so we should not simply treat these years as preparation for their future life.

Second, the future is rapidly changing and unpredictable. It is very difficult to predict what the future will be like. There is no pre-made future waiting for children to walk into. In fact, the future is co-developed with children, and when they become adults, they play a major role in determining their life. The attempt to prepare children for the future is, at best, an attempt. Instead, what is important is to help children develop the capacities for creating a better future when they grow up and to help them work with uncertainties and unknowns.

Third, the idea that education in one grade is preparation for the next grade is fundamentally flawed. Schools may have a grade-level based curriculum and assessment that they must follow, but in reality how much people can learn during one year can vary a great deal. Schools try to homogenize that learning by following a curriculum. While a student can learn much more or less than a school actually teaches, the school tries to control what a student learns within its physical or virtual walls. Students who cannot keep pace with the curriculum are placed "at risk."

Furthermore, in educational systems where year-level assessments are mandated for certain subjects, students are forced to study whatever will be assessed. As a result, a student can be seriously held back by the curriculum and assessment. A student who is ready to learn at a level way ahead of what the next year holds still has to wait. Likewise, a student who is not keeping up academically has to be pushed to do more or else be left behind.

More important, today students can learn on their own from sources outside of school. Given the rapid development of technology and online learning resources, a student technically can learn anything from anyone online, without the instruction of schoolteachers. It means that students' learning is no longer bound to the instruction provided in a school. It also means that schools do not have to teach everything students wish to learn.

The Recipient Mindset

Another dominant mindset that supports the school pathway believes that students are recipients of education. There is a common belief that students cannot learn without being taught. School is also built on the idea that students must be managed and disciplined by adults. As a result, students are placed in classes and taught by teachers.

This mindset is, of course, wrong. Students can learn on their own when given the opportunity. Children—and all human beings— are capable of learning (Bransford et al., 2000; Mitra, 2007, 2020; National Academies of Sciences, Engineering, and Medicine, 2018). They need exposure to the information; they need to interact with the information; they need to have the opportunity to practice and think about the information; and they need to reflect on the information. People can learn by being taught, watching videos, reading books, or playing with others. Learning via being taught is just one way of learning. Furthermore, given the abundance of online videos, courses, and learning communities, students can certainly learn without being taught by a teacher in their school.

If we can let go of both the Preparation Mindset and the Recipient Mindset, we can begin to imagine a new school pathway, one made possible by the following factors.

New Forms of Learning

While schools remain the dominant form of formal learning, other forms of learning have emerged. These new forms of learning do not have to have a teacher who teaches a group of students in the classroom. They can be done with little resources or with a lot of resources. The core of the forms of learning is the autonomy of the learner.

Redes de Tutoría ("Tutoring Networks") in Mexico is a great example. In many ways, *tutoria* is like any one-on-one tutoring session. The tutees have great autonomy. They can choose what interests them from a list of inquiry-based projects. They then approach a tutor, who gives them a tutoring session. Upon completion of a topic, the tutee becomes a tutor, who can provide tutoring to others. This approach has been very successful in parts of Mexico where access to highly qualified teachers has been challenging. It has also been adopted in Chile, Thailand, Peru, and Argentina (HundrED.org, 2020). In the words of Harvard education professor Richard Elmore, who has studied education for over four decades,

> In my view, tutoria occupies a very special niche among the exemplars that will guide the future of learning. Tutoria is special in a number of powerful and informative ways. It is a practice that is designed to lead to the development of a progressively more complex and deep theory of learning, driven by the practice itself. The practice is relatively simple; the theory leads to increasingly powerful and complex understandings of how young people and adults learn. In this sense, it reverses the traditional social science relationship between theory and practice, and it creates a culture that is organized around what I would characterize as "deliberate surprises." The

practice emphasizes questions rather than answers. The essence of the tutorial relationship is to give as much control as possible to the learner over the choice of what to learn and to structure the tutorial relationship around the learner's discovery, through a dialectical process with the tutor, of how a body of knowledge works—not just what knowledge is, but how and why it takes the form it does. It stresses reasoning and discovery over fluency and speed in finding right answers. (Elmore, 2016, p. 3)

Other very important aspects of *tutoria* that Elmore has praised include the applicability of the approach in any situation. Elmore commended *tutoria*'s "complete indifference to physical environment" because he has seen it "work in the most deprived physical settings, consisting of only the bare minimum shelter, with minimal light, and bare dirt in the outdoor learning spaces." He has also seen it work in places where there are Wi-Fi and computers as well as places where a computer is not in sight. He has seen it work in dangerous places as well as safe environments. It works in all kinds of environments, because "the power of the practice does not come from the accoutrement of the physical environment; it comes from the deeply personal and powerful learning practice and the theory of learning it embodies" (Elmore, 2016, p. 4).

Large-Scale Learning Environments

Large-scale learning environments have emerged with the advancement of technology. In general, these learning environments involve a massive number of users/learners. The users can be both teachers and students. They are both contributors and consumers of content at the same time. These environments have entered the lives of billions of people—children and adults. Youths have been actively utilizing them, although sometimes more for purposes of entertainment than for purposes of learning.

Large-scale learning environments are extremely diverse. They include massively open online course (MOOC) platforms, collaborative programing communities, intelligent tutoring systems, social learning networks, collaborative gaming systems, social media systems, and fanfiction sites. These environments have different characteristics and can be used in different ways for a variety of learning purposes.

Take fanfiction sites. Cecilia Aragon and Katie Davis, two University of Washington professors, documented the amazing learning process and outcomes of fanfiction sites in their book *Writers in the Secret Garden: Fanfiction, Youth, and New Forms of Mentoring* (2019). These sites are massive. One of them, fanfiction.net, has more than 7 million stories and 176 million reviews contributed by more than 1.5 million writers, most of whom are in their teens and twenties. Cecilia and Katie discovered that these sites are sophisticated online learning spaces that demonstrate the power of *distributed mentoring*. The sites have contributors with different experiences and expertise but who all are committed to writing, reviewing, and building support for each other. The mentoring that the members provide to each other can be of different styles and approaches, but it does greatly help them learn and grow. I interviewed Katie about this phenomenon; you can access the video from http://bit.ly/learnerswithoutborders.

Of course, the other large-scale learning environments, such as MOOC platforms, intelligent tutoring systems, collaborative gaming systems, and even platforms such as YouTube, provide tremendous space for learning. For example, Khan Academy, a website that offers all sorts of free learning for students from the age of two all the way to beyond college, has served millions of people (Khan, 2012). Scratch, a visual programming language and website that aims at giving children a global space to learn how to program and play online, has over 50 million users in school and after school around the world (Resnick, 2017). With large-scale learning environments continuing to develop, it is not an overstatement to say that if someone wants to learn something—anything—he or she can do so today.

Questioning the Value of College Education

Going to college is one of the primary driving forces of the school pathway. Many students want to go to college, and society has generally promoted the idea that going to college will somehow guarantee a better life. Attending college has become an accepted and privileged social position for many families. While college may still have tremendous intellectual, economic, social, and psychological value, there has been increasing concern about whether all should go to college and the declining value of a college degree (Freeman & Hollomon, 1975; Freeman, 1980; ProCon.org, 2020).

It is clear that future workers will need higher levels of skills than high school has traditionally offered. But it is also clear that people can obtain such skills without spending four years and hundreds of thousands of dollars in college. Besides the opportunities provided through large learning systems, and besides the skills that people can develop on their own, there are other providers. For example, Google recently announced the Google Career Certificates program (Walker, 2020), which aims to become a pathway to jobs. The Google Career Certificate website states that "certificate completers can directly connect with a group of top employers" and completers will qualify for jobs "with median average annual salaries of over $50,000" (Google Career Certificates, 2020).

Some people in positions of power have opposed traditional college education. For instance, the billionaire Peter Thiel, cofounder of PayPal and investor in Facebook, has established a fellowship program to discourage students from attending college and, instead, help them pursue their own ambitions. Thiel has argued that "he could do a better job than degree-making institutions by giving bright, ambitious adolescents and young adults the freedom to reach for loftier goals" (quoted in Clynes, 2017). "College can be good for learning about what's been done before, but it can also discourage you from doing something new," counsels the Thiel Fellowship website (Thiel Foundation, 2011). The $100,000 per person fellowship offers a stipend and opportunities for mentorship, business guidance, and networking. The idea is to help the fellows chart a unique course. The Thiel Fellowship program believes that "together they have proven that young people can succeed by thinking for themselves instead of following a traditional track and competing on old career tracks" (Thiel Foundation, 2011).

NEW PERSONALIZED PATHWAYS

Rejecting the Preparation Mindset and the Recipient Mindset will help change our thinking about the school pathway. When schools are not preparing children for the future but focusing on providing the opportunity for every child to be engaged in a meaningful life, students will no longer need to be moved as a cohesive group along a curriculum framework. When schools begin to accept that students can learn on their own without being taught by a teacher, they can be allowed to learn in ways that do not require them to be in a classroom.

The new forms of learning and the large learning systems provide examples of different forms of learning possibilities. Students no longer need to be taught directly by teachers. They can and they do learn from each other. They can also learn from online courses and resources.

Going to college is not necessarily for everyone. But not going to college does not mean one should stop learning. Instead, there are other options that enable young people to learn and become employable.

Individual, Unique Pathways

We are living in an era in which whenever a person wishes to learn, he or she can. Instead of viewing groups of students following the same process toward graduation, we can instead consider every school as a school of one. That is, the school can look at every student as the only person the school serves. For that purpose, the school, in essence, builds a unique pathway for each and every student.

A student would develop this pathway in collaboration with teachers and parents (Zhao, 2018c). Ideally, all students in a school can decide, in collaboration with adults, what they want to learn (Zhao, 2012, 2018c), but the reality is that many schools still have to implement a required curriculum, which makes it impossible for students to decide completely their own learning. We'll discuss curricula more in Chapter 5. Regardless, it is possible for schools to adjust the curriculum and courses to provide students with a certain degree of latitude to follow their passions and develop a unique knowledge base. In other words, a school can require students to take certain courses, but the school can also allow students enough space to exercise their autonomy and self-determination (Wehmeyer & Zhao, 2020). This, of course, requires the school to bring in resources from outside to support each student.

When every student has a unique pathway, students do not need to follow the same curriculum and take the same courses at the same time. They can move faster or slower. They can take higher or lower courses, unrestricted by their age. They can count other courses or activities, such as entrepreneurship, as part of their own learning pathways. They can also take college-level courses while in school, thanks to online learning platforms such as Coursera and edX. They can also enroll in the Google Career Certificates program.

Student Grouping

School leaders should also reconsider student grouping. There is absolutely no good reason to organize students into classes based on their age, although it has been the most common practice. It has become very clear that children are diverse and different in all aspects (Zhao, 2018c). They have different physical appearances, different cognitive potentials, different personalities, different dreams and aspirations, and different social and emotional status. More important, children reach different levels in each domain at different times, for various reasons. For example, some children are able to read at a much younger age than other children. Others are more socially mature than their age peers. Thus, students of the same age do not necessarily have the same state of development and learning.

Moreover, students may vary in their strength in each domain. One student might be way ahead of his peers in math but quite behind in reading. Likewise, a student might be three or four years ahead of her peers in reading but at the same level as them in math. A student may be quite more socially mature than his peers but behind in physical growth. Thus, it is difficult, if not possible, to judge students' abilities based on their age.

Finally, even assuming all children were exactly the same in all areas of development and learning, any way to organize students based on age would include one year of differences because schools enroll students on an annual basis. In other words, a school that takes in students born between January and December would have one year difference among the students; so would a school that takes in students born between August and July. There is no way to remove this difference.

Multi-age grouping places students of different ages in the same classroom group. A multi-age classroom can typically take students with two to three years of age difference. A teacher or a group of teachers typically teach the group for at least a year or more. This is a hallmark arrangement of the well-known Montessori approach.

This arrangement has been said to have several benefits. For example, the students can be with the same teacher(s) longer, which gives the teacher(s) more opportunity to develop a deeper understanding of the students and thus places the teacher(s) in a better position to support the students. Older children can also serve as mentors for younger students, and such interactions are typically considered educationally beneficial to both groups. In mixed-age or multi-age groupings, children are more easily viewed as unique individuals than in homogenous classrooms, which often apply the same expectation to all students. Multi-age classrooms also give children more time to learn, because the children do not need to spend time getting to know their teacher or their classmates. When new students are added to the classroom, there are plenty of students who have already formed a community for them to join.

There has been much research about the benefits, or lack thereof, of multi-age grouping (Ervin et al., 2016; Shalom & Luria, 2019; Veenman, 1995, 1996). Early research did not find significant difference in terms of cognitive achievement, but multi-age grouping students have better attitudes toward school and themselves (Veenman, 1995, 1996). In recent years, studies have found that multi-age grouping appears to be better than homogenous grouping in terms of students' academic achievement and social-emotional learning (Ervin et al., 2016; Shalom & Luria, 2019).

Ability-based grouping is another way to group students. In multi-age grouping, students are in the same group for multiple years, and teachers teach the same group. In ability-based grouping, students are allowed to choose the class that matches their ability in different domains. For example, a student who has a high reading ability can choose to be placed in a higher-level reading class rather than in the class of his age peers. If the same student's math ability is lower than that of his age peers, he can choose to be in a lower math class.

Ability-based grouping is different from *ability grouping*, which has been in practice in education for a long time and has resulted in quite inconsistent outcomes (Buttaro & Catsambis, 2019; Ireson & Hallam, 2001; Park & Datnow, 2017; Slavin, 1987; Steenbergen-Hu et al., 2016). The most significant difference is that ability-based grouping involves allowing students to select the courses they desire to take, across grades or age levels, whereas ability grouping typically involves sorting students of the same grade/class into different ability groups. Ability-based grouping gives students autonomy and agency, while ability grouping is something that is done *to* students.

Ability-based grouping is not practiced much in many schools; thus, it is very difficult to find research about its effectiveness. We can, however, imagine that when students are permitted to pursue their interests and take courses that match their abilities, the effects cannot be that bad. More important, enabling students to pick and choose their courses beyond the confines of their age group gives them the opportunity to exercise their self-determination, to practice agency, and to have access to the right content, which is beneficial for learning.

SUMMARY

The school pathway has long been a dominant way of living for children and youths. It is extremely difficult to imagine a different way of living and learning than schooling. However, it is possible, and it is students who may have to take action in this regard first.

Teen entrepreneurs, for example, do not need to go back to school. They can just take care of their businesses and work on learning to make them better. They can learn from their local communities. They can learn from others online. They can take courses on MOOC platforms. They can form their own online learning communities. Not finishing school when their age peers do does not mean they cannot get a college education if they wish to later, although higher education is going through major changes as well. They can, if they wish, work on getting the equivalent of a college education.

Students do not have to learn only from what schools offer or be limited to what schools can offer. They can learn from external resources, their peers, and online courses. They can learn through actively investigating or developing solutions to important issues in the world. They can collaborate with people from nearby or faraway. The most important thing is that they want to learn.

Schools can help in this process. They can create new options for students. These options include allowing and enabling students to create their own learning pathways, which can include external resources, personal experiences, and other forms of learning. Schools can also make significant changes to how they group students for purposes of instruction. Schools do not have to *teach* as much as they have been. School leaders should look at how they can help each and every individual student become successful rather than how well they produce good test scores or implement the required curriculum.

After all, learning has now proliferated beyond schools. Schools may still control credentialing learning, but the school pathway is not the only means of success!

CHAPTER 5

Breaking the Curriculum Border

"[Students] are planning their futures on the belief that doing well in school creates opportunities—that showing up, doing the work, and meeting their teachers' expectations will prepare them for what's next," according to New Teacher Project report (TNTP, 2018, p. 2). "They believe that for good reason: We've been telling them so." The report goes on:

> In short, students and their families have been deeply misled. We talk about school as a series of small opportunities for students—to show up, work hard, earn good grades—that add up to much bigger ones later in life. When students don't find the opportunity they were promised on the other side of the graduation stage, we assume they or their families must have done something to blow their big chance, or that they were simply reaching too high. (TNTP, 2018, p. 5)

The report is a scathing analysis of schools today, especially in how schools prepare students for better opportunities in the future. It is based on a study of five school districts around the country with nearly 1,000 full-length class observations, 5,000 student assignments reviews, more than 20,000 student work samples, and 30,000 student surveys. The study found that students have high aspirations and big goals. And while most students do what they are asked in school, they are still not ready to succeed after school.

The study found that 88 percent of the time, students were working on activities related to class. Seventy-one percent of the time, students met the demands of their assignments. Over half of the students received As and Bs. However, students demonstrated mastery of the grade-level standards only 17 percent of the time. In addition, on average, students "spent more than 500 hours per school year on assignments that weren't appropriate for their grade and with instruction that didn't ask enough of them," which in essence means "six months of wasted class time in each core subject" (TNTP, 2018, p. 4). Not surprisingly, students were not very engaged with their courses. They reported that their school experiences were engaging just 55 percent of the time. The number is only 42 percent for high school students. The report blames the lack of engaging experiences on low expectations from teachers. "We found that while more than 80 percent of teachers supported standards for college readiness in theory, less than half had the expectation that their students could reach that bar" (TNTP, 2018, p. 4).

FUTILE EFFORTS

The situation described in the report is not new or unknown: Schools are not preparing students well. But the report highlights one very important thing—that the students are following what schools and teachers teach them very well. They "show up, work hard, and earn good grades." And yet they are still not prepared for the future. They are not ready for college and careers.

The report highlights "an urgent need to authentically engage students and families in creating paths that honor the aspirations, talents, and needs of each student" (TNTP, 2018, p. 50). In recognition that "a lot of 'innovation' continues to fall short of our basic promise to students," the report offers a solution:

> No matter what the tagline, any curriculum, program, or model that does not allow students consistent opportunities to engage with grade-appropriate assignments, to do the thinking in their lessons, and to engage

deeply with what they are learning is effectively perpetuating the opportunity myth. Good intentions aside, if we aren't giving all students those opportunities regularly, we are systematically denying them the chance to even try to master the skills they need to reach their goals. (TNTP, 2018, p. 50)

In other words, the problem with American schools is lack of access to four things: grade-appropriate assignments, strong instruction, deep engagement, and teachers with high expectations. The first three issues are actually all symptoms of the fourth: students are not held accountable to high expectations. There are two recommended solutions:

> Every student should have access to grade-appropriate assignments, strong instruction, deep engagement, and teachers with high expectations, every day, in every class—regardless of their race, ethnicity, or any other part of their identity.

> Every student and family is an authentic partner and should have real opportunities to shape the experiences students have in school, receive accurate and accessible information about students' progress, and have a legitimate role in decision-making. (TNTP, 2018, p. 56)

The recommendations are not necessarily new, either. High expectations and uniform expectations of students have been the approach recommended and turned into policies in the United States and many other countries (Zhao, 2012). Fixing schools by fixing the curriculum and then assessment has almost been a standard in the world. The United States, for example, has had No Child Left Behind (2001) and then the Common Core State Standards (2010), followed by the Every Student Succeeds Act (2015). The basic idea is to have high curriculum standards and high expectations for all students. The same has happened in Australia, with its movement to a national curriculum. In the United Kingdom, similar efforts were made in developing its new curriculum standards and expectations.

The reform efforts in various countries that have focused on changing curricula, instructional materials (textbooks), and teaching methods do not seem to have worked well. For example, since the issuance of the Common Core State Standards (CCSS) in 2010, thousands of school districts have adopted new curricula and textbooks intended to align with the new standards. A large study by the Center for Educational Policy Research (CEPR) at Harvard University found that over 80 percent of schools in six states use elementary math textbooks aligned with CCSS. About 93 percent of teachers reported using the textbooks in over half of their lessons (Blazar et al., 2019). In essence, these districts have changed their curricula to align with CCSS, changed their textbooks—ostensibly carrying higher level of expectations—and changed their instruction in the classroom, but without much effect.

The CEPR researchers examined students' academic outcomes in six Common Core states. They looked at fourth- and fifth-grade test scores during the three academic years from 2014 to 2017. The findings were disappointing:

> Overall, we found little evidence of differences in average achievement gains for schools using different math textbooks. We also did not find impacts of textbooks for schools where teachers reported above-average levels of textbook usage, for schools that had been using the text for more than one year, or in schools that provided an above-average number of days of professional development aligned to the textbook. (Blazar et al., 2019, p. 1)

The study essentially shows that textbook and curriculum changes do not have a significant impact on students' outcomes. "At current levels of classroom implementation, we do not see evidence of differences in achievement growth for schools using different elementary math textbooks and curricula" (Blazar et al., 2019, p. 1), but it leaves some possibilities: "It is possible that, with greater supports for classroom implementation, the advantages of certain texts would emerge, but that remains to be seen."

This study may or may not be conclusive. It is difficult to imagine that curricula and textbooks do not matter to students' learning. If they don't matter, why do we spend millions of dollars developing them? And there are a few other studies that show impact of textbooks in some areas as well, but they are fairly small studies compared to this one. Improving curricula, instructional materials, and teaching should be valuable. Two of the authors of the

CEPR study, Thomas Kane of Harvard and David Steiner of Johns Hopkins University, wrote an op-ed in *Education Week* after the report's release (Kane & Steiner, 2019). The commentary's title, "Don't Give Up on Curriculum Reform Just Yet," communicates their intention very well. They do not want to close the book on curriculum and instruction:

> Contrary to our (perhaps naïve) hopes, we have learned that curriculum materials alone are not enough. But the worst thing we could do now would be to conclude that teaching rigorous, demanding academic content to *all* our students can't work. By systematically identifying the package of supports that teachers need to make full use of stronger materials—and by attaching student achievement gains to textbooks so that publishers have an incentive to provide the supports teachers need—we can make progress. To close the book on curricula now would be equivalent to closing the book on learning. Curriculum is the foundation for what students and teachers do together every day. (Kane & Steiner, 2019)

THE OWNERS OF CURRICULUM

In the broadest sense, a curriculum includes everything students experience when going to school. It is the formal curriculum taught in classes. It is also the extracurricular activities students can choose from. It is the rules and regulations that students and school staff need to obey. It is the school culture that students and staff have in common. It is the intended curriculum—that is, things people do and experience. It is also the hidden curriculum (Giroux & Penna, 1979)—that is, lessons students learn but which are not intended by the curriculum. These lessons can include, for example, the transmission of cultural values, norms, and beliefs through classrooms and the school environment.

Given the paramount importance of a curriculum in learning, we must ask two questions. First, who owns the curriculum? That is, who creates the curriculum for students to experience? Second, who should be the owners of the curriculum? In other words, who has the right to create the curriculum for students to experience?

Governments

Governments are currently the most influential body in curriculum making. Although educational systems differ around the world, the role of governments in making the curriculum for students rests with some level of government. In the United States, states dictate the standards that schools (and therefore students) must abide by, but the development and choice of curriculum is often up to individual districts or schools. The federal government has little power in creating the curriculum, but it has played a role in state standards through various education laws and special programs such as the Common Core State Standards. In Canada, the body that makes the curriculum is the provincial government. In Australia, the national and state governments create the school curriculum together.

Governments should have the right to make curricula, because they provide the funding for schools. They are the funders of schools in their capacity to represent the people, because the funding comes from taxes paid by the people. So, in many ways, the curriculum created by a government represents the people's will and desire. Thus the curriculum represents what the people want future generations to know and be able to do. The curriculum represents traditional cultural values, the knowledge and skills of the community, and the knowledge and skills needed for success in the future.

Schools

Schools are where the curriculum is realized. Some educational systems, such as the United States', allow schools to create part of the curriculum. In China, the central government, provincial government, and the local school each develop part of the curriculum. The central government creates the core for every student in the entire country. The provincial government creates part of the curriculum, and the local school creates the rest.

Whereas schools are often not the primary curriculum creator, they still play a significant role in implementing the curriculum. The intended curriculum must be realized in schools by school staff. Besides staff, schools should also have the infrastructure, facilities, and social organizations to translate the curriculum into daily activities for students. Thus, schools play a significant role in the curriculum students actually experience. The daily activities that students experience in school are, in essence, the implemented version of the intended curriculum, which is the curriculum made by governments.

Schools also play a significant role in defining the hidden curriculum for students. The local culture of each school matters tremendously to the school environment and to relationships between students and staff as well as relationships between students. Moreover, schools also define in-school extracurricular activities, such as student clubs, sports, and other after-school programs.

Teachers

Teachers do not create curricula, but they are perhaps one of the most important implementers of the curriculum. Their personality, knowledge, skills, understanding of the curriculum, and intention to implement the curriculum affects how they realize the curriculum in their lessons. Their knowledge of and attitudes toward students and knowledge also impact their classes. Teachers are the direct contact point for students to interact with the formal curriculum. In addition, teachers can play a significant role in defining the informal curriculum and affecting the hidden curriculum.

Textbook and Software Publishers

Textbooks or packages of instructional materials also play a role in defining curricula indirectly. Although publishers are not directly involved in making a curriculum, they interpret the curriculum or multiple curricula from different states. They then embody their interpretations into textbooks. They also can provide training to teachers to influence their interpretation and uses of the textbooks and software packages.

Test Publishers

The role of assessments in affecting curriculum implementation cannot be overestimated. It is widely accepted that teachers and schools "teach to the test." Test publishers—especially those who develop accountability tests for schools and tests for college admissions—matter tremendously for students, teachers, and schools. Schools and teachers can adjust the implemented curriculum—for example, by reducing time and efforts for untested subjects or content and increasing time and effort for test subjects and content in instruction. Students can also choose to focus only on the test subjects or content.

It is apparent that the curriculum students experience is influenced by many actors in the educational system. But the students, the owners of learning, are largely outside the curriculum-making and -implementation process. This is largely because of the traditional view of students and curricula. Traditionally, students are viewed as recipients of a great curriculum that is age-appropriate and ready for the future. So their job is to show up, work hard, and follow the teachers who follow the curriculum. When students who follow this prescription are not successful, then teachers are blamed, schools are blamed, and students are blamed. The curriculum, the intended curriculum, the one that is designed for students to become successful, can also be blamed and can be changed as well.

THE MISSING ACTOR

"Curriculum is the foundation for what students and teachers do together every day" is a powerful statement. Indeed, curriculum is what every school offers to its students. As a concept, curriculum has many meanings (Kelly, 2009). It can be a body of knowledge to be transmitted, or it can be an attempt to achieve certain ends in students (Smith, 2000). It can also be a process through which learning takes place, or praxis—"an active process in which planning, acting and evaluating are all reciprocally related and integrated into the process" (Grundy, 1987, p. 115). Whatever the definition, curriculum is what all students experience in school.

Thus, efforts to improve curriculum are not necessarily wrong. However, just changing the curriculum won't improve education. In fact, simply making curriculum more challenging and demanding does not improve education. Changing instructional materials and instructional approaches to align with higher levels of curriculum does not work, either. This is why reform efforts in the United States, Australia, and the United Kingdom have not yielded significant changes over the past few decades in terms of domestic assessments and international assessments (Wehmeyer & Zhao, 2020; Zhao, 2018c, 2018e).

These reform efforts' foremost failing is their general negligence of the most important factor in learning: the learner. In none of the reform efforts were students highlighted as change makers in the process. Students have been generally viewed as passive recipients of educational reform efforts and their consequences rather than as active partners. Even as the recipients of education, students have been considered a homogenous group instead of a collection of unique individuals.

Neglecting students as a factor of change poses several challenges to improving the quality of education (Wehmeyer & Zhao, 2020). First, students are the learners. No matter what educational plan is made, students are the ones who are supposed to experience and benefit from it. Thus, unless students are actively engaged in the change process, what is given to them is like any curriculum or materials their predecessors have received. The new curriculum to them is just a curriculum. There is no special meaning to it. The students would not feel much difference. As the New Teacher Project study shows, students believe in school. They follow the teachers, they show up, and they do the assignments (TNTP, 2018). However, if students had been involved as partners of change (Zhao, 2011), they could be much more active in pushing the changes as well. They could change their behaviors and change their attitudes toward the reform efforts.

Second, students are extremely diverse in many ways (Zhao, 2018c). As a result of interactions between nature and nurture, or innate attributes and experiences (Ridley, 2003), people develop different interests and passions, acquire different skills and knowledge, and hold different attitudes and values. When they are students, they have different academic achievements not only in terms of their test scores in different subjects, but also in terms of their capacity for learning different subjects. They also have varying levels of interest in different subjects. Furthermore, they have different personalities, which can drive them to be interested or uninterested in certain aspects of school. Moreover, their age does not measure their abilities or interests. As a result, even when grade-level-appropriate materials are presented to a group of students, they are not grade-level-appropriate for all students of the same age. The materials can be too high or too low for some and just right for others. In other words, whatever curriculum is presented to a group of students, it is not appropriate for a subset of them. The same is true for instructions.

Third, the reform efforts still have the view that one curriculum works for all students. The reformers have been working on improving curriculum and teaching, but the basic idea is still to have one curriculum—or set of standards—for many students. Their view is that there is one curriculum or set of standards that can prepare all students for success after they finish school.

But that belief is largely a fantasy. First, the future is very uncertain and is constantly defying our predictions. It can be affected by many expected and unexpected factors, such as economics, politics, technology, and health issues. It is therefore impossible to accurately forecast what jobs will or will not exist when today's elementary-school students enter the workforce. If we cannot predict the kind of jobs that will exist, it is impossible to determine one curriculum to include all the knowledge, skills, and capabilities needed for the future. Second, the future is not pre-made by someone for our youths to walk into. In fact, we don't ever prepare our children for future jobs; *they*, as participants of the society, participate in making the future, including its jobs. Third, the number of college majors and specializations is in the hundreds, if not thousands. And different majors and specializations have different expectations of students and rely on different sets of foundational knowledge and skills. There is no single curriculum that can meet the demands of hundreds of majors. Fourth, there are over 4,000 colleges and universities in the United States alone. These institutions differ from each other so much that they cannot possibly be expecting students to have the same set of knowledge and skills transmitted through one all-purpose curriculum.

Educational reforms that are developed without involving learners can hardly succeed. This is why students can show up, work hard, and get good grades but still fail to flourish after graduation. The percentage of students intending to go to college is high, and many schools have been successful in sending students to college. But the percentage of college dropouts has been on the rise as well. Today, about 40 percent of college students do not get their degrees in six years (Kirp, 2019). There may be many reasons for students to drop out of college, but not having been well prepared for the majors and specializations is surely one. The reasons for their not having been well prepared include the ideal of one curriculum for all students.

STUDENTS AS CO-OWNERS

For any educational changes to be successful, we must change curriculum. But the change must not involve only content or structure; it must also involve who *owns* the curriculum. We cannot persist in imagining students as simply the recipients of the curriculum. Students—as the ones who experience the curriculum, who live the consequence of the curriculum, and who bear the outcomes of the curriculum—must become its owners as well.

Owning the Curriculum

The first step in helping students own the curriculum is to start personalizing the curriculum for each person. In other words, a school should offer not one curriculum but as many curricula as there are students. Each student should have a unique educational experience in school. In this way, students will experience school not only as prescribed by governments, schools, and test, textbook, and software publishers. Instead, they will be the co-owners of their own curriculum with these others.

There are many ways to achieve curriculum personalization. But it is important to point out that personalization of the curriculum is different from personalized learning automated by technology. This personalization is not only about how fast, when, or how students learn, but also about what students learn. It is much more than the process of learning. It is also about the purpose of learning. The purpose of learning is to not only transmit what society wants students to learn, but also to develop students' unique abilities to succeed in life (Zhao, 2012; Zhao & Tavangar, 2016).

It is also important to point out that the process of creating a personalized curriculum for each student is also a process of actively engaging students to take responsibility for their own learning. In this process, students are not assigned a curriculum. Instead, they work with adults, teachers, and parents, each semester or each year, to accept what is required of them in the curriculum standards or curriculum, to select what they may be interested in, and to come up with courses or learning opportunities that are unique to them. The students then manage their curriculum, experience the curriculum, assess their learning, and continuously modify the curriculum.

Elements of the Personalized Curriculum

To personalize the curriculum for each student, we must understand that the curriculum each student experiences should have at least three parts: the core, the elective, and the personal. The core curriculum—or, in some cases, standards—is what every student must learn. It is typically created by the government or an authoritative body. The curriculum contains the most basic knowledge and skills related to the cultural norms and values that a society wishes its future generation to pass on. It also contains the most basic knowledge and skills the society deems necessary for students to become good citizens. The core is for the common good, common understanding of the society, and common practices and values of the community.

However, currently the core is too big in many societies. It takes up all learning time for all students. There is little room for school or students to add anything of their own to the curriculum. Thus, the first thing to do in order to personalize the curriculum is shrink the core curriculum.

Besides the core curriculum, a school or school district should have its own signature curriculum for all its students. A physical school is located in a certain community, which may have its own social expectations, cultural values, laws and regulations, or other significant common issues that it expects all students to become familiar with or learn about. A school also should have its own cultural identities and academic uniqueness. The size of the school curriculum can vary, but, in general, it should be small, perhaps around 20 percent of the instructional time.

Electives are curriculum content that students can choose as part of their personalized curriculum. Electives can be part of the government- and school-mandated curriculum, but they are not mandated for all students. These courses can be used to cover certain domains of content and skills mandated by the government and/or school curriculum. The electives should be mapped onto students' interests and strengths.

If government-mandated curriculum takes 30 percent of a student's curriculum and school-mandated curriculum takes 20 percent, the rest should be personal curriculum. That is, about 50 percent of the student's curriculum should relate to knowledge and skills the student wishes to pursue. This is possible even with students as young as elementary school age. While the specific percentages may vary in different situations, it is important to have students suggest things they wish to learn and make them part of the curriculum.

The personal part of the curriculum should help a student develop a unique pathway of success. It should be built on the student's interest and passions, to expand his or her strengths. This part of the curriculum should be completely driven by the student, in collaboration with adults.

It may be difficult to imagine how students know what they wish to learn. Some may not even believe that students know what they wish to learn. But that is not true. By the time students come to our schools, they have already been exposed to an abundance of experiences. They have watched TVs, played with smartphones and tablets, interacted with their friends and parents, visited museums and/or libraries, and perhaps even read books. Their experiences have given them the basis of interests or passions. They certainly have an idea of in what areas they would like to learn more, know more, or do more. Even if they didn't know what they would like to learn, teachers could work with them to stimulate their interest.

In summary, a personalized curriculum should have three parts: the government-mandated, the school-mandated, and the personally contributed. The entire curriculum should contain what the society desires its future citizens to know and be able to do, what a school decides its students should become, and what individual students can become based on their interests, desires, passions, and abilities. The curriculum also includes the "floor" curriculum, which is what every member of the society should know and be able to do, as well as the "success" curriculum, which is the personal curriculum of the individual student. The success curriculum contains the abilities, knowledge, aptitudes, and other abilities that make a person unique based on his or her passions and strengths (Zhao, 2018c).

Implementing a Personalized Curriculum

Curriculum personalization is not a new idea. It has been practiced in Democratic Schools (Greenberg et al., 2005; Grenyer, 1999; Stanford, 2008), as well schools that follow the Reggio Approach, which promotes an emergent curriculum for students to co-develop what they learn. Variations of curriculum personalization have also taken place in public schools. Templestowe College, a government school in Melbourne, Australia, has engaged in personalization of student curricula. Students at Templestowe have great autonomy in what they learn and how to learn (Zhao, 2018c; Zhao, Emler, et al., 2019). Monument Mountain Regional High School in Massachusetts once allowed a group of students to run their own "school" within the school, essentially allowing the students to create their own curriculum (Levin & Engel, 2016; Wehmeyer & Zhao, 2020).

Schools can take different approaches to implement personalized curricula. First, the percentages suggested here (30% government-mandated, 20% school-mandated, and 50% personal) are not meant to constrain a school, in particular when a school is just getting started in changing. The different parts can be bigger or smaller, but it is important to give students sufficient space to exercise their right to self-determination in their curricula. That is, students must be given ample time to follow their own curricula.

Second, curriculum personalization should take place in all levels of school. It should not be deferred until high school. Some educators may believe that young children should all learn the same thing in order to be ready for personalization later. But young students have a strong interest in pursuing their own passions and are very creative in their thinking. Thus, they should be supported to pursue their interests and passions with personalized curricula from the start.

Third, working with students to create personalized curricula should be a significant part of schoolwork. Creating the curriculum is a process of learning and should not be considered just preparation for learning. Having teachers work with students to explore and identify their interests and strength is itself a learning process for students. This process benefits the students for life, because it touches the core of learning by helping individuals discover what they want to learn and why they want to learn. This requires schools to reconsider the purpose of education and seriously examine what they offer to students. It builds a healthy and reciprocal relationship between students and teachers as well.

Fourth, schools must be able to provide opportunities and resources to support the various ways in which students want to expand their knowledge and skills. There are lots of ways to grow the opportunities that include students teaching or mentoring each other. The different levels of knowledge and skills that exist among a diverse population can be a great learning resource. Students can be invited to offer optional courses for each other, which is what students at Templestowe College did (Zhao, 2018c; Zhao, Emler, et al., 2019). Or they can provide mentoring sessions for their peers, like the Redes de Tutoría tutors in Mexico (Elmore, 2011, 2016). Students and teachers can also bring in online learning opportunities. They can participate in MOOCs, use open education resources (OER), join international learning projects, or access web resources such as Khan Academy. There are experts, expert institutions, and organizations in local communities that can be of help as well.

Fifth, supporting curriculum personalization requires big changes in the teacher's role. Teachers' primary role in this arrangement is that of personal consultant to students. They work with students and parents to uncover and stimulate students' interest and passions. They help students understand the possible outcomes of different combinations of courses and learning activities. They advise students on what possibilities and courses are a fit for them. They also help promote students' talents to others. Teachers are also resource curators. They identify online and local resources for students; they evaluate and manage resources for students; they can also recruit and attract resources. Additionally, they teach small classes, work with small groups of students on projects, and help build a healthy learning ecosystem for all students.

Finally, the most important actor of a personalized curriculum is the student. The student needs to accept the role of managing his or her learning. This is a dramatic change from the typical school experience, where students show up and comply with the school-assigned learning experiences. Instead, the student is actively managing his or her learning experience in collaboration with adults. The student is engaged in a continuous process of reflecting on the learning experience, discovering new interests and opportunities, expanding his or her capabilities, increasing his or her understanding of content, and developing new skills.

Not all students have the motivation and skills to develop and manage their own learning right away. It takes a collaborative effort between the school and family to help children develop such capabilities and skills for self-determination. However, there are plenty of strategies for promoting students' ownership of their own learning, and we now know a lot about students' desire for self-determination. The most important thing for schools to do is start giving students the space and support (Wehmeyer & Zhao, 2020).

SUMMARY

Educational reform efforts around the world have been focused on changing the curriculum for students, making it more challenging, more age-appropriate, and better delivered. However, the efforts are still aiming at creating one excellent curriculum for all students. Schools are still working on training teachers to parse and implement a single curriculum for all students. These efforts cannot possibly improve education for all students, because of the diverse backgrounds and diverse capacities and interests of a large group of students. In addition, students live in different communities, with different schools and cultures. The qualities of schools differ vastly across a single state or nation, let alone across the world.

What needs to change is our focus: we must shift the focus to students. First, schools need to accept students as the rightful co-owners of their curriculum. Then, schools need to work with students to develop a personalized curriculum for each and every student. The personalized curriculum should have three components: government or system-mandated curriculum, school-mandated curriculum, and personal curriculum. This requires governments and systems to make their existing curriculum smaller and reflect only the most basic "floor" expectations of the society. The students' curricula are what makes them unique and great. Finally, schools need to shift the attention from teaching a prescribed curriculum to supporting students' exploration of their own curricula.

This is the only way to enable students to break away from the curriculum border.

CHAPTER 6

Breaking the Classroom Border

One of the consequences of the COVID-19 pandemic, which shuttered millions of schools for over a billion students worldwide, was that all students and teachers gained experience with remote learning (Gigova & Howard, 2020; United Nations, 2020). Whenever possible, when schools were closed, schools attempted to provide students a continuous educational experience using remote learning. While the formats of remote learning varied a great deal—from online courses to TV and radio broadcasts—the experience of learning outside school was common to all students and teachers.

The remote learning experience may not have had equal outcomes all the time for all students, but it helps make the point that learning does not have to happen in the classroom. This common experience should be the starting point of rethinking education—in particular, how it has been delivered in traditional classrooms.

In traditional schooling, learning is usually delivered and managed by a teacher in the classroom. The teacher teaches the prescribed curriculum content to a group of students. The teacher may or may not utilize outside resources, but the most important element is that the teacher delivers instruction and the students follow the teacher as a group. Students are stuck in the situation. They have to be in the classroom. They need to do what the teacher tells them to do and comply with all the rules made for the classroom. They must also learn what the teacher teaches, although they may already know the content or be way behind the content. There is no way that a student can escape from the classroom.

But the COVID-19 pandemic let students learn outside the classroom. At the time of writing this book, for different durations, students have experienced remote learning. They have learned in various ways. Some have learned by following the traditional class schedule, watching their teacher's instruction synchronously with their classmates located in different places. Some have watched TV broadcasts together with tens of thousands of their peers and then had synchronous lessons with their own teachers and classmates. Some have had great freedom to follow their passions and checked in with their teachers only occasionally. Some have explored their own interests with very limited contact with their teachers. Still, some have basically enjoyed being allowed to do whatever they like.

These diverse yet remote learning experiences have given students a taste of learning that is not classroom-based. Even those students who have had to follow the school schedule and followed their teacher's instruction have had a different experience. There have been no other students sitting beside, behind, or in front of them. There has been no group of students with them physically in the same location. There has been no teacher watching them all the time. There is a screen between them and the teacher. In some ways, distance learning has given students more control over their learning environment.

Remote learning has also given teachers the opportunity to try something different from the traditional classroom. Millions of teachers have taught differently, without much preparation or professional development. Even for those teachers who simply moved their classes online, the teaching was still different. Teachers were forced to use technology, to find the broadcast location, and to consider their presentations. Unlike in a classroom, where teachers can see all students, teaching online makes it impossible for teachers to have a quick view of what each student is doing. It also limits the teachers' capacity to interact with students. In the classroom, a teacher can use many different ways to interact with specific students while giving lectures. For example, they can move closer to a student who is not engaged. They can use their hands to direct certain students sitting in front of them.

The variations of the remote learning programs during the COVID-19 pandemic did not give all students and teachers the same quality of experience, but—if nothing else—it should have given teachers and students a different perspective of learning and teaching: that learning and teaching can take place outside the classroom. This is a simple and obvious truth but has often been forgotten in schools, where the default view of education has been that learning and teaching take place inside an isolated classroom.

COVID-19 helped break the default view of education. It gave students and teachers learning and teaching experiences so drastically different from the traditional classroom. These experiences teach us several important lessons about education: First, classrooms are not the only place learning can take place. Second, teachers are not the only source of information. Third, lecturing is not the only way to teach. Fourth, learning can be completely reorganized.

THE CLASSROOM IS NOT THE ONLY PLACE FOR LEARNING

Classrooms have been the default place of learning for a long time: If you want to learn something, you go to school. When you are in school, you are placed in a classroom with your peers. When you are in a class, your teacher instructs and you learn. You listen to the teacher, follow his or her instructions, and do your homework. You learn with your peers and progress as your peers do. It is rare for students to learn outside of this rigid system.

There are many reasons that learning is usually confined to the classroom—chief among them that the teacher has been considered key to learning, as mentioned before. The teacher bears the responsibility for knowing what students need to know and for being able to teach the students what they need to know. In other words, if a student wants to learn something, there must be a teacher to teach him or her. But for reasons of efficiency, a teacher must teach more than one student at a time. Hence, a teacher must be located in one place where more than one student can gather around him or her to learn. The place is the classroom.

Things began to change in the 1990s, when the Internet became widespread. Prior to the internet, there had been many attempts to promote remote learning and distance education. In the 1920s, Thomas Edison tried to use films to replace teachers and textbooks. "I think motion pictures have just started and it is my opinion that in 20 years children will be taught through pictures and not through textbooks," Edison was quoted as saying (Associated Press, 1923). Films did not exactly replace teachers or textbooks. Later on, radio was believed to bring the revolution—but again, it did not. Television was also believed to have the potential to replace teachers and textbooks. Despite the efforts to offer education on TVs and radios, the majority of education still has not been changed. Classrooms, with teachers teaching a group of students, have remained.

The evolution of the Internet over the past three decades brought something different. The digital format replaced the traditional analog format and, thus, was able to combine and mix all traditional forms of media (Negroponte, 1995). This global network connected all digital devices, such as traditional digital computers, together to allow transmission and exchange of files. The arrival of "smart" devices made it possible for virtually everyone to have access to remote information. The Internet has also resulted in the massive and ubiquitous social media that connect billions of individuals together. More important, what the Internet connects is not only access to information but also access to experts and the ability for interactions.

Today, the changes the internet has brought have already massively transformed society. It has made the "gig economy" possible. It has displaced human workers from millions of jobs and ended traditional industries. It has changed how we live, socialize, and entertain.

The changes brought much excitement in education as well. There was much expectation that education would be greatly disrupted (Christensen et al., 2010)—education would be open, and online education would become mainstream. Indeed, there had been big changes in education before COVID-19. Massively open online courses (MOOCs), open education resources, online schools and programs, and numerous forms of globally accessible instructional modules, micro-credentialing programs, and synchronous instructional sessions had served millions of students (Bonk, 2011; Bonk et al., 2015).

However, schools have not been fundamentally changed by all these developments. By and large, most K–12 students still go to school and attend classes the same way their parents and grandparents did. One teacher still dominates the classes. Schools still operate the way they always have. Even during the COVID-19 pandemic, when schools were closed, many parents, teachers, education leaders, the general public, and governments wanted schools to return to "normal," by which they meant the way things used to be.

This, however, does not mean school should be the way it has always been. Neither does it mean that today's technology cannot change schools (Zhao et al., 2015). It only means that the "grammar of schooling" (Tyack & Cuban, 1995; Tyack & Tobin, 1994) is very solid and strong. In a seminal paper published in 1994, education historians David Tyack and Larry Cuban pointed out that schools' operation appears to be governed by a set of rules, akin to the grammar of language. These rules dictate how schools operate: Knowledge is splintered into school subjects, subjects are taught by a teacher, school time is divided into class periods, and students are organized into classes. The "grammar" of schooling makes the school a school and accepted as a school in society. It has been very persistent. Despite many meaningful efforts to change it over the past hundred years, it remains.

The "grammar" of schooling was seriously challenged by COVID-19. Although the virus did not change the grammar of schooling, the school closures forced learning to take place outside school. This was the first time in the history of education that all schools across the globe were impacted by the same phenomenon. This worldwide closure of schools made it possible for millions of students to experience learning outside the classroom. During the closure, which differed in length for different jurisdictions but ranged from four weeks to more than twelve months, students had access to remote learning materials, attended remote classes, collaborated with remote partners, and completed homework remotely. Students essentially had a taste of learning beyond the classroom. The learning may still have been orchestrated and managed by a teacher, but it is undeniable that students did not experience it inside a classroom.

The COVID-19 pandemic has made major industries change how they operate. Numerous businesses have changed their office-centric culture and have begun to allow their staff to work from home or moved toward a hybrid model of working—with staff working at home remotely and coming to offices for necessary meetings. Facebook, for example, announced that it would allow many of its staff to work from home (Conger, 2020). Google has decided to allow its staff to work from home but decided to make offices places for gatherings during days when staff come together (Hartmans, 2020). But schools seemed to have refused to rethink their spaces. They were eager to return to the same buildings as soon as COVID-19 was reasonably controlled (in some cases, even when the virus continued to spread).

Accepting the idea that learning does not have to be in the class-room seems difficult, but it is inevitable. As discussed earlier, the internet and related technologies have made it possible for teachers to reach their students, for students to attend classes, for students to interact with their peers and teachers, and for students to gain access to numerous online resources. Students can and did conduct learning outside the classroom during COVID-19. If a student can learn outside the classroom, education can be organized very differently.

THE HUMAN TEACHER

Teachers have traditionally been viewed as the only source of information and managers of students' learning. Teachers have been held as the individuals responsible for students' learning. Traditional educational reforms have often focused on holding teachers accountable for their students' academic achievement. Recruiting, training, and retaining high-quality teachers have been major strategies for improving education.

But teachers are no longer the only source of information. Although teachers still have the authority inside the classroom as the managers of students' learning, the sources of information students can learn from have vastly increased. Students can easily have access to online videos of instruction, online discussion groups, and online tutoring if they wish. Students can also take classes online from other instructors. That is, if a teacher allows it, students can learn from numerous resources.

This is, however, not to say that we don't need teachers anymore. Quite the contrary; we still need teachers to teach students, albeit in a different way from lecturing or instructing. Instead, teachers should focus on building relationships with students and supporting their learning. In other words, technology can facilitate teachers' adoption of a more uniquely human role (Zhao et al., 2015).

In *Never Send a Human to Do a Machine's Job* (Zhao et al., 2015), my coauthors and I made a strong case that teachers and technology work together in the ecosystem of education. Teachers should not be competing with machines. Instead, they should work with technology, delegating to technology the things that they cannot do, don't want to do, or are unable to do. Following this advice, teachers should examine their own work and actively allow technology to relieve them of the work they are not supposed to do.

For example, a teacher is not nearly as efficient as technology to show the eruption of volcanoes or massive disasters. Teachers should allow students to watch videos of these events instead of talking about them. Teachers are unable to bring tours of remote museums to the students, but technology can do that very well. Teachers are also unable to become the live audience of students' works, but technology can connect students to possible audiences remotely. Furthermore, it is not the best thing for teachers to spend time on correcting multiple-choice exercises or repeating their lectures. If a teacher can find videos of recorded lectures of their intended content, there is no reason for him or her to recreate them. If a teacher can record and reuse his or her own lecturing for later use, he or she should do so. Overall, a teacher should not teach anything that can be found on the Internet.

When examining their work in this way, teachers may realize that their best job does not involve "stand and deliver" lectures in front of an entire class or grading all students' homework. Much of what they do should be different. When students can learn content and skills from online resources, their teacher should not be simply giving them the resources. Students can watch on their own. When students can learn the content through interactive software, their teacher should not be just observing. When students can learn by interacting with their peers and experts beyond the classroom, their teacher should not be simply standing by.

NEW FORMS OF TEACHING AND LEARNING

It is time to change teaching. When students can learn beyond the classroom and the teacher is no longer the only source of learning, teaching should change.

There have always been different ways of teaching. In 1894, renowned educator John Dewey (1859–1952) founded a school within the University of Chicago that had an approach to teaching and learning very different from that of traditional schools (Tanner, 1997). The school started as a grand experiment. The intention was to help students grow emotionally, socially, and intellectually. To ensure that students' prior experiences were connected with their present lives and that learning was active and cheerful, the school took the following measures (Knoll, 2014):

- The teachers were group leaders. Their responsibilities included creating an environment resembling a loving family.

- Time and resources were allocated for supporting self-activity and self-expression.

- Students took on individual and collective undertakings in various places, such as kitchen, laboratory, studios, and workshops.

- The learning activities were focused on practical problems and activities that reproduced typical situations of social and communal life.

Known today as the University of Chicago Laboratory Schools, or simply Lab (UCLS, n.d.), Dewey's school was among the first to put the students at the center of learning and bring the world into the school. Students were engaged in actively constructing a community with adults, and the learning was done by doing.

Other methods have taken a similar approach. These approaches typically are called inquiry-based learning, project-based learning, problem-based learning, exploratory learning, or discovery learning. While their names differ, the forms of teaching all have five common features. These features create a different form of learning that places the student at the center of the learning process.

The most important feature of new forms of teaching and learning is that *students are treated as active learners*. In the traditional model of learning, students are considered as passive recipients of instruction. The forms of new teaching and learning treat students as active explorers who are engaged in investigating and discovering laws of the natural world and rules of the social world. They learn by finding answers and creating solutions to problems. The learning is guided and led by the students.

The second feature is that learning is *purposeful*. All learning should be intentional and serve a purpose instead of passive memorization of knowledge or meaningless compliance.

In the early days at Lab, for instance, learning did not start with reading, writing, or arithmetic instruction. Instead, students were engaged in activities such as cooking. During cooking, students would need to reference cookbooks, which was an opportunity for them to engage in reading. They would also need to write about the characteristics of the food they prepared, which called for the exercise of writing (Knoll, 2014).

Thus, learning to read and write served the purpose of deciphering cookbooks and recording students' actions.

Third, learning is *authentic*. Learning should come from authentic experiences, solving authentic problems, and creating authentic products. "Authentic" means real, genuine, and not fake or pretend. Learning experiences that are authentic are experiences that are grounded in genuine, real-world problems rather than artificial, made-up problems. Authentic learning experiences are multidisciplinary and provide rich opportunities for learning a wide variety of skills and knowledge. Reading, math, science, history, arts, and many other subject matters can be infused in authentic learning experiences.

Fourth, learning should be about *uncertainty and unknowns.* The purpose of new forms of learning is to help students develop the capacities to work in uncertainty and unknowns, instead of teaching them the known answers to known problems. Memorizing existing solutions to previously identified problems does not help students come up with creative solutions to the uncertain and unknown, which has become the reality today.

Fifth, teachers' roles have changed in the new forms of learning and teaching. Teachers are *facilitating, leading, and supporting* instead of lecturing. Teachers are not dominating the class or disciplining students. Instead, they work with students as consultants, facilitators, and group leaders. They may give lectures to an entire class when necessary, but they spend most of their time with individual or small groups of students.

TECHNOLOGY AND TEACHERS' ROLES

The new forms of teaching and learning started when the power of technology was fairly limited. When Dewey started Lab, there was no Internet, which means no websites, YouTube, or social media. Dewey brought kitchens, workshops, and studios into the school so that students were able to work with authentic products and tools. But students were not able to watch videos, listen to podcasts, search for information, talk with people globally, use sophisticated software, or create and share products around the world instantly.

Over a hundred years later, the power of technology is drastically different. Technology has transformed not only how we live, work, entertain, and socialize, but also how we learn. It is not an overstatement that, if allowed to, today's schools can be drastically different from schools in Dewey's day. As supporters of hybrid or blended learning (C. R. Tucker, 2020) would attest, technology, when properly used in schools, can bring entirely different forms of teaching and learning. It can dramatically improve the new forms of learning. Teachers can blend various online and offline resources in their teaching. But, most important, they can help students design and develop their learning plans, which includes resources from various places.

The entrance of more powerful technologies in education has made it necessary to go beyond the question of what teachers should do. Although new forms of teaching and learning—as practiced in Lab, in project-based learning, in inquiry-based learning, and in authentic learning—made teachers change their roles, technology can do more in shifting teachers' roles in the process, for four main reasons.

First, today's technology can do a lot of things that teachers do. For example, the most important thing that teachers do in class is instruction or explaining the content. That can be done and has been done by technology. Besides the Khan Academy, there are numerous videos of great masters of content explaining the content of K–12 curriculum. There are also numerous online courses or instructional modules for students to watch and learn from.

Second, intelligent tutoring systems and other instructional software further enhances the possibility of learning without direct instruction by the teacher in the classroom. Intelligent tutoring systems, for example, with the support of artificial intelligence technology and big data, can interact with individual students and learn about their habits and abilities and the deliver personalized learning to them without the involvement of teachers. The variety of educational software or apps is simply amazing. They cover materials starting as early as kindergarten, and some are quite effective.

Third, today's technology can easily connect students with experts and peers beyond the classroom, globally. It expands students' access to not only expertise but also potential collaborators. This possibility, again, makes it unnecessary for teachers in the classroom to be the only expert. More important, it frees students to learn with people from far away.

Fourth, today's newest technology moves past consumption to focus on creation. It enables users to create and share their content broadly. Thus, students can be powerful media owners, multimedia authors, software developers, app designers, and members of large online communities. They can and do create content to share it online. They have the potential to reach millions. This can dramatically change the power structure in the classroom. What happens in one classroom does not stay in the classroom anymore. It goes global.

The power of today's technology is difficult to reckon with, but every teacher must confront it. COVID-19 has forced every teacher to deal with technology but not necessarily to rethink their relationships with technology in the classroom or remote teaching. A good way to think about the relationship is "never send a human to do a machine's job," a line from the movie *The Matrix* (1999).

The power of today's technology is difficult to reckon with, but every teacher must confront it.

This line was used as the title of a book my colleagues and I wrote (Zhao et al., 2015). In this book, we examined five top mistakes in the field of educational technology. The top mistake is the replacement theory, which argues that technology would replace human beings and other technologies. The theory is partly right in that new technology can replace certain functions of old technology or capabilities of human beings. But it does not necessarily replace the old technology or human being. For example, digital reading devices can hold books and other reading materials, but they do not necessarily replace print books or newspapers.

Instead, new technology can redefine the functions and roles of technologies and human beings. For instance, television did not replace radio but moved radio out of the living room, to cars and other places. The Internet did not replace television but drastically reduced its role in family life. Despite loud calls or predictions that technology such as film, radio, and television would replace teachers, it has not happened and perhaps will never happen.

The challenge in education, then, is not so much about whether technology will replace teachers, but what aspects of teaching will be done through technology and what aspects have to be done by teachers. In other words, aspects of teaching or certain functions of the teacher must be replaced by technology. However, the replacement is only partial. When technology enters teaching, a teacher must consider what he or she should do.

The challenge in education, then, is not so much about whether technology will replace teachers, but what aspects of teaching will be done through technology and what aspects have to be done by teachers.

The answer lies with "never send a human to do a machine's job." The teacher should not always play the role of an instructional machine that pipes knowledge into students' minds. The teacher should be more human. Thus, instead of competing with technology, the teacher should retreat from what the technology does.

Following this advice, we can posit that teachers should not do three types of things. First of these is things that technology can do but human beings cannot do. It is extremely difficult for teachers to facilitate collaboration with students in other schools, or even across the globe—but technology does so easily. Second, teachers should allow technology to do things that they don't want to do. Again, there are many things that technology can do that teachers may not want to do. In traditional teaching, there are many tasks that are repetitive and boring— for example, grading simple assignments with right or wrong answers. There is no reason for teachers to do these tasks. Another example would be memorization of words when learning a foreign language. Many teachers often use flashcards to help students in this regard, which can be accomplished much more easily and effectively by having students use computerized flashcards or online programs on their own.

Third, technology sometimes can do things more efficiently or at less cost than teachers. There are tasks that teachers *can* do but could be done more efficiently with machines. Teachers may enjoy doing them, but technology does a better job. For example, teachers may enjoy lecturing to the class, but recording the lecture or finding online recordings and having students watch them in small groups may be more effective and provide more opportunities for peer collaboration and individual conferences with students. Lecturing to a class often misses the top and bottom levels of students. Having students access the recorded lectures on their own can greatly enable learning, as demonstrated in the Flipped Classroom movement (Akçayır & Akçayır, 2018; B. Tucker, 2012).

Teachers are at their best when they take care of the human aspects of education, which may wind up neglected when teachers have to spend most of their time studying the curriculum, studying the subjects, preparing for instruction, and delivering the instruction while managing the classroom. But when teachers follow the new forms of teaching and learning and make thoughtful use of technology, their teaching changes; so do their roles (Zhao, 2018a).

Life Coaches

One of the most important roles teachers can play in education is that of life coaches. A life coach tries to understand a student as a person, to know the student's strengths and weaknesses, to appreciate the student's passions and desires, and then to help the student see possibilities. As life coaches, teachers also help their students connect their unique strengths and passions with the real world. They support students' pursuit of their passions and develop their unique strengths. Most important, they look at their students as individual human beings who have different personalities, different dreams, and different capabilities. They do not question the value of these differences. They believe everyone's uniqueness is valuable and work to help each and every student become better and find places they can shine.

When teachers assume the role of life coaches, they build deep relationships with students. It is well known that healthy and human relationships with students are key to students' success. When students are treated as equal members of a community and have strong relationships with teachers, they are motivated and engaged. They are proud and eager to engage in learning activities and aspire to do more and better.

Curators of Resources

Another role that teachers should assume is that of curators of learning resources. There are vast amounts of information and numerous learning materials and experts online. But not all of it is appropriate for all students. When teachers, as life coaches, understand their students' strengths and passions, they know their needs and should spend time curating online resources and tools in order to help their students develop their strengths and pursue their passions.

Curating resources for each and every student is not an easy job. It requires a teacher to understand where each student is and what that student's strengths and passions are. It then requires the teacher to find and evaluate technology-based resources and resources in the school and local community. The teacher must work closely with each student and that student's parents/guardians to fashion a set of usable resources for the student. Curated resources make it possible for each student to pursue a personalized learning journey.

Community Leaders

Teachers have another role to play—that of leader of the learning community. A class of students forms a learning community, which can operate many smaller learning communities. The learning is social and interactive. Students, as members of this community, are in constant interaction with each other and also with resources and people from outside the community. These communities can be collaborative project teams. Teachers are leaders of this community, in collaboration with students.

Communities operate with rules and regulations, so teachers need to lead students to create such rules and regulations for collaboration. Teachers and students should also work together to design and develop activities and events for their learning community. Communities have unique identities that need to be developed with the leadership of the teacher. Furthermore, communities live within larger communities and interact with other communities. To ensure unique identities and productive relationships with other communities, teachers need to provide leadership as the community defines itself.

Project Managers

Finally, teachers need to become project managers. When learning becomes personalized and project-based, management of projects and individualized learning plans becomes very important. A teacher needs to support students, especially younger ones, to learn to manage their own personal learning plans, to help them develop self-determination skills so that they can become self-determined learners (Wehmeyer & Zhao, 2020). Moreover, when students are engaged in project-based learning, the teacher needs to help all students manage their projects well and ensure progress.

As project managers, teachers must have a set of capacities that are different from those required in traditional instruction. Project management skills are different from giving lectures and disciplining a class. To manage projects, teachers need to develop skills in understanding project times, progress, and motivating participation. They need to develop skills in communication and skills in moving the projects forward. In addition, they need to become the person who praises progress, supports the slow movers, and ensures good spirit. They also need the ability to support demonstration of projects to the public and ensure broad support from the community.

SUMMARY

Learning has been constrained in the classroom for a long time, with the teacher as the sole learning provider, but the teacher does not have to be the dominant character in the classroom today. As discussed in this chapter, the ubiquity of technology makes it possible for students to learn directly from numerous online resources. It also makes it possible for teachers to pre-record their lectures and/or use software for students to learn. Moreover, it enables students to learn from peers in other schools and other lands.

The COVID-19 pandemic forced schools to offer remote learning to students. Virtually all teachers have participated in offering remote learning to students, proving that teaching and learning can be done outside the classroom. Furthermore, it gave many teachers the experience to recognize that they are no longer the only source of information in the classroom.

When teachers recognize that teaching and learning are no longer constrained to the classroom and they are not the only information source, they should recognize that education can go through major transformations with the help of technology. The first major transformation is for them to actively use technology to bring in online educational resources and software to release them from lecturing or instructing the entire group of students. The second major transformation is for them to engage their students in authentic learning with technology so that their students are constantly finding and solving worthwhile problems. The third major transformation is for them to expand the learning environment globally, to engage students in global collaborative projects so that their students are working with peers and experts from beyond their classroom. The fourth major transformation is for them to work with students on individual learner profiles in their new roles as life coaches, resource curators, community leaders, and project managers. The final major transformation is for teachers to become more human and to see students as individual human beings rather than recipients of content from the curriculum.

These transformations would help break the classroom border, which limits students' learning within the classroom. They would help our students move beyond what their local teachers can offer, help connect our schools with the real world, help bring the real world into our schools, and help send our students into the real world prepared.

CHAPTER 7

Self-Directed Learners

"Self-advocacy" was the answer Kanoa Hirschmann, a senior student at Mid-Pacific Institute in Honolulu, Hawaii, gave to my question, "What would make students the owners of their own learning?" on Episode 29 of *Silver Lining for Learning* (Yong Zhao, 2020). This episode was about students' voices in education. We had three students as our guests, including twelve-year-old Tex Mikkelson from Australia. Our conversations primarily focused on educational innovations during the COVID-19 pandemic. It was clear that what the students praised most was the possibility of owning their own learning.

Owning one's own learning sounds like a paradox. Students are the learners, and they should be the owners of their own learning. But in too many schools, that is not the case. Students have been typically going to school to receive an education designed by and for someone else. Rarely have students been involved in designing and deploying the learning experiences they have in school.

They need advocacy to fight for ownership of their learning. They must be determined to navigate through what their school offers and find what they need for their own learning. They have to negotiate with school leaders and teachers to create a set of courses for themselves. Students can do this when they have developed the mindset that they do not work for school; school works for them. This is when they have become aware of their own right to learning.

But schools do not always respond to students' advocacy. Too many schools are proud to offer students a very strict plan of learning, with very well designed courses, clearly defined outcomes, and a tightly controlled pathway of progress for all students. Students in these schools are asked to follow the curriculum, pass the exams, and complete their tasks. Hardly anything can be altered. Students rarely have any voice or choice over the core curriculum the school offers, let alone own their own learning.

This is why Emanuelle Sippy, another twelfth-grader who joined our show, said we need to change our systems. Emanuelle represented the Prichard Committee Student Voice Team, consisting of over one hundred students from elementary school through college who work as education research, policy, and advocacy partners to improve education in Kentucky. Emanuelle emphasized the great need for schools and educational systems to create space so that students are able to own their learning, as well as the need at a system level to enable students to take ownership of their learning.

Changing the school pathway and breaking the prescribed and predetermined boundaries of curriculum and classroom requires students to take ownership of their learning. Unless and until students are ultimately the owners of their learning, learning will still be controlled by curriculum authorities, the traditional grammar of schooling, and teachers who hold control of students. So far, we have mostly discussed the possibilities of changes by curriculum authorities, school leaders, and teachers. In this chapter, we discuss the students' role.

NATURAL-BORN LEARNERS

One of the most common questions I have encountered when proposing that students should be the owners of their learning is whether students *can* learn on their own. There seems to be a general view that students do not want to learn and that, unless tightly controlled or carefully instructed, students will not learn.

The assumption is that, if given more control, they would not know what to learn or how to learn. And, on the surface, the widespread phenomenon of student disengagement seems to back up this view. It is not uncommon for many students to not pay attention in class, choose to skip school, or decide to drop out of school. Thus, classroom management strategies, motivational strategies, and various ways to stop students from dropping out have become much needed for teachers and schools.

But, in reality, students are natural-born learners (Beard, 2018; Gopnik, 2016; Gopnik et al., 1999; Smilkstein, 2011). As human beings, we are all born learners, which is the only way we can survive in the world. Our natural survival strategy, unlike other species', is our capacity for learning, for creating strategies and tools to deal with the outside world. Every one of us is born with both the necessary desire and ability to learn new things. In other words, learning is the only way for babies to survive and thrive:

> Every child is a passionate learner. Children come into the world with a desire to learn that is as natural as is the desire to eat and move and be loved. Their hunger for knowledge, for skills, for the feeling of mastery is as strong as any other appetite. They learn an amazing variety of things in the years before they enter school, including, miraculously, how to talk fluently in their native language. And they continue learning at a terrifically high rate throughout their childhoods. (R. L. Fried, 2001, p. 124)

There is little question that children want to learn, and they do learn amazingly complex things during very early years. They learn to understand the complex world. They learn to understand and participate in building and maintaining human relationships. They learn math, science, and language. They learn about cultural values and social norms. From the perspective of learning, no one would be able to dispute that children are indeed natural-born learners.

However, things change when they come to school, the place that is supposed to offer an experience of learning. In his book *Natural Born*

> Every human being is born with both the necessary desire and ability to learn new things.

Learners: Our Incredible Capacity to Learn and How We Can Harness It, Alex Beard, after documenting how human beings are natural-born learners and babies are scientists in the crib, made the insightful observation that "our models of education are too often limiting [the human superpower to learn]" (Beard, 2018, p. 299). In his view, education works to frame "our minds as computers to be fed information" and reduce "learning to a program of inputs and outputs" rather than unleash our native ability to learn.

As a result, after they spend some time in school, many children begin to lose their excitement about learning. Around third or fourth grade, passionate learners become compliant students, and their zest for knowledge continues to dissipate as they progress. Although not all students lose their passion for learning, the phenomenon of disengagement is widely observed. Despite teachers' efforts , students become much less fascinated and less eager to learn what school has to offer them.

DIVERSE LEARNERS

Why does children's passion begin to dissipate when they are in school? Scholars and educators have proposed various answers. They have also developed strategies to keep students motivated and engaged. Yet the situation has not changed significantly. The motivational strategies have worked to some degree but have not eliminated the problem of disengagement. Various approaches to keep students engaged and in school have also ameliorated the problems but have not made all children passionate learners.

The real reason behind the disappearance of passion in school has never been addressed. The reason is the conflicts between diverse students and homogenous expectations of schooling. Students come to school with diverse innate abilities or aptitudes, different personalities, different passions and interests, and of course very diverse experiences as a result of their home and community backgrounds. But school, as the institution to educate all children, has only one set of expectations, one mode of operations, and one set of rules. As a result, there is an inevitable conflict between the diversity that exists among students and the homogeneity expected in school.

The diversity among students is the result of complex and sometimes random interactions between nature and nurture (Lewontin, 2001; Ridley, 2003). Students are born with different intelligences (Gardner, 2006), different personalities (John et al., 2008), and different desires (Reiss, 2004, 2008). These inborn traits are boosted, or suppressed, or simply ignored by the diverse experiences that young children have as they grow. As innate learners, children are constantly in the process of learning, which, in essence, is a process of nature interacting with nurture. As a result, they have different knowledge, skills, aptitudes, personalities, passions, interests, attitudes, and values when they arrive at the school door.

These differences affect how well they do in school. Because schools offer a relatively set number of courses/subjects, they cannot possibly cover everything that diverse students want or are good at. As a result, some students are extremely good with the school subjects; others are extremely bad at them. And some others can follow along. Likewise, some students may be extremely eager to learn what their school offers, and some may be interested, but some others may hate the subjects.

Moreover, the speed at which students learn the subjects varies a great deal. Schools tend to have a homogenous view not only of what to learn, but also of the rate at which it should be taught. As discussed in Chapter 5, schools and educational systems abide by grade-level expectations, usually established by standards or a curriculum. That is, they expect students of a certain age to be able to do certain things and know certain things. This expectation does not work, because children are intentional and diverse human beings. Imagine that some students already read fluently upon entrance to school, while other students had never been exposed to print before they come to school. How could these two groups of students move along the same pathway? Also imagine some students who love to read and others who hate the idea of reading. How can these two groups of students achieve the same level of reading by the end of first grade?

The homogenization approach to teaching a diverse body of students is the primary reason that students lose interest in school. Almost all children are excited to go to school, and that's what is expected of them as well. But as soon as they arrive, many discover that what they are interested in and good at may not be valued in school. They cannot learn what they want to learn. Some students either are good at and interested in the school subjects or possess a great work ethic and an interest in complying; the rest of the students play along, pay no attention, cause trouble, or drop out as soon as possible.

> The homogenization approach to teaching a diverse body of students is the primary reason that students lose interest in school.

The homogenization approach has been in practice for a long time, and there were good reasons for that in the past (Zhao, 2012, 2016). In the Industrial Age, the majority of the workforce needed to have similar skills and knowledge but without necessarily being great and excellent (Zhao, 2018c). The situation has changed. Because most traditional jobs already have been or will be replaced by automation in the Fourth Industrial Revolution, what is valuable now is unique greatness and humanity. Human beings need to have an education that supports the diverse strengths and passions of all students.

Such an education is unlikely to occur without advocacy, as our twelfth-grader Kanoa suggested. Even within the existing systems, students who can advocate for their own needs can possibly have a better education. They might follow the example of Samuel Levin, who led the effort to build a school within a school for himself and a small group of fellow students in his Massachusetts high school (Levin & Engel, 2016). However, it has been rare to see students asking their teachers and school leaders to customize education for them. And even if students do ask, rarely do schools agree (Zhao, 2018c; Zhao, Emler, et al., 2019).

SELF-DETERMINED LEARNERS

Why don't students fight for their right to learning? Why don't students argue for their ownership of learning? Do students want to own their learning? These questions are worth asking because they represent another fundamental question in deciding the future of education. If students did not want to own their learning and pursue their own path to success, it would not make any sense to promote it.

Self-determination theories have long established that we humans desire self-determination (Ryan & Deci, 2017; Wehmeyer & Zhao, 2020). We actively seek control of ourselves and our environments. We want to exercise the right of determination over what we do and experience (Wehmeyer & Zhao, 2020). The three natural tendencies that we human beings have—(1) autonomy, (2) competence or mastery, and (3) relatedness—are all related to being able to control ourselves and our environments.

Autonomy is the innate desire to be the causal agent of one's own life, consistent with one's integrated self (Deci & Vansteenkiste, 2004). Everyone wants to be able to follow his or her own will and volition without being coerced by external agents. Much research in psychology supports this notion. For example, it has been found that extrinsic rewards can undermine intrinsic motivation (Lepper et al., 1973). It has also been found that the many extrinsic incentives to promote reading did not have great impact on students' reading (McQuillan, 1996). Taking away autonomy can negatively affect intrinsic motivation. Human beings seek to take action within their own control. They prefer that their actions and behaviors be the results of their own decisions instead of external factors.

Competence or mastery is our desire to seek control over the outcomes of our actions and experience mastery. We have a basic need for competence, and, thus, our intrinsic motivation increases when we are praised. We want to be able to learn, to improve, to become better, and to master. We are in deep need of accomplishment, out of our own ability and efforts.

Relatedness is our desire to be able to relate to others, to care for and be cared for by others. Humans are social animals. We need relationships. We want to be able to contribute to other people's lives, and we want our lives to be influenced by others.

Self-determination is not only psychologically supported as a basic human need, but also a basic human right that should not be violated. In 1989, the United Nations passed the *Convention on the Rights of the Child* (United Nations, 1989), which has become the most widely ratified international treaty. This convention specifies that children under the age of eighteen have the human rights to be self-determined, to have autonomy, to have the ability to take control of their own life. For example, Article 13 says,

> The child shall have the right to freedom of expression; this right shall include freedom to seek, receive and impart information and ideas of all kinds, regardless of frontiers, either orally, in writing or in print, in the form of art, or through any other media of the child's choice.

Article 14 says "States Parties shall respect the right of the child to freedom of thought, conscience and religion." What is of particular interest is the statement toward the end of Article 29. Articles 28 and 29 are both about states' responsibility to provide education for all children and say that education should be directed to "the development of the child's personality, talents and mental and physical abilities to their fullest potential" and "the development of respect for human rights and fundamental freedoms."

We cannot build educational institutions to interfere with the liberty of individuals and we cannot sacrifice individual liberty in the name of education. Education, in most places in the world, consists of formal schooling, which has often been used as a way to control individuals and to make them espouse certain political or religious views. Education should not be brainwashing!

THE LOSS OF LEARNING

It is apparent that students are diverse, self-determined, and natural learners. We want to learn, and we do learn. We are born owners of our learning: We decide what to learn, when to learn, and how to learn in interactions with our parents (guardians) and our environment. We develop strengths and weaknesses. We develop passions and interests, and we arrive at school diverse and different. We arrive at school with all intentions to learn and exercise our rights to self-determination.

This is a great foundation upon which to build an educational system in which learners have more freedom, in which they can truly learn without the traditional school pathway and the curriculum and classroom boundaries. There is little reason that learning should be confined to a local school, the constraining curriculum, and the isolated classroom.

However, the great basis of learning without borders is lost on schools. The model of education practiced in most schools today works very well to make students lose their passion for learning. By offering one set curriculum, schools force students to study things they may not be interested in or good at, as discussed in Chapter 4. Students are also judged by a single set of criteria, which can make some students feel like a failure constantly. Students who have other talents and are not good at the school subjects may have no opportunity to demonstrate and be recognized for their talents.

Moreover, schools have a set of predetermined ways to operate. Students have very little to no space and time to experience autonomy, competence, and relatedness. Because the school's primary task is to ensure that the students are learning what is prescribed, the entire school time is occupied by pre-planned lessons and teaching. The entire school campus has also been preset. There is very little that students can influence or change. The only thing they can do is follow instructions and do what teachers tell them.

Furthermore, schools, as a system, reward compliance. Standardized testing or traditional grades often favor those who are willing to learn the prescribed content and perform well on tests and school-required tasks. School disciplines and traditional expectations of behavior also favor those who are willing and able to comply while punishing those who behave differently. As a result, even those students who have talents in and passion for areas outside school subjects are willing to sacrifice those talents and passions for school subjects and school disciplines.

Last but not least, traditional approaches of instruction in the classroom, such as direct instruction, can seriously damage students' passion for learning and desire for self-determination. Research has found that direct instruction may give us a form of "unproductive successes," in which learners may show short-term gain of the content but at a cost to their curiosity and creativity. Moreover, direct instruction causes students to rely on their teachers, lose self-dependence, and lose critical thinking skills (Zhao, 2018e).

Schools, as they are, essentially serve to make children lose their desire to have control of their learning life and their actions. They also aim to homogenize the diverse set of learners cognitively, in terms of what to learn, and social-emotionally, in terms of how to behave in school. As students spend more time in school, they lose their passion for learning and learn to suppress their desire for self-determination.

TEACHING SELF-DETERMINATION

A common observation when schools try to implement programs to liberate students, to make them owners of their own learning, is that some students are reluctant to participate or do not know how to take ownership. This is not surprising, if students have been inundated in traditional schooling. Students, after spending many years learning to comply with school demands and receive education from teachers, have learned that they really don't have the option to exercise their right to self-determination—or they have lost the intention, the desire to gain control of their own learning. It is also possible that they have learned from their experiences that schooling is an enterprise in which self-determination is not needed for success.

We can help students regain their desire for self-determination. In our book *Teaching Students to Become Self-Determined Learners* (Wehmeyer & Zhao, 2020), Michael Wehmeyer and I offer a whole set of ideas about teaching students to become self-determined learners. The first thing we need to do is acknowledge that students are natural-born and self-determined learners. But their school experiences do not allow them to exercise their right to self-determination. As a result, they gradually lose the innate desire. To teach self-determination is to help students regain the right.

Second, there are different frameworks for promoting students' ownership and determination of learning. The overarching message is to teach students to teach themselves. In self-determined learning, students "learn how to set and advance goals and make plans, to be agents of their own learning" (Wehmeyer & Zhao, 2020, p. 35). This requires teachers to "relinquish ownership for learning to the student, not by abdicating all roles in teaching but by creating learning communities and using teaching methods that emphasize students' curiosity and experiences" (Wehmeyer & Zhao, 2020, p. 35).

Specifically, certain teaching methods can focus on supporting the development of autonomy, competency, and relatedness:

> These methods are autonomy-supportive and ensure that learning is tied to activities that are intrinsically motivating or lead to the attainment of meaningful goals and that are based on student preferences, interests, and values. Teachers provide competence supports by emphasizing mastery experiences, using assessment to provide supportive feedback, and by aligning instruction with students' strengths and abilities. Teachers provide relatedness supports by providing choice opportunities, supporting volition, and emphasizing the goal process not just goal outcomes. (Wehmeyer & Zhao, 2020, p. 35)

Some of the characteristics of autonomy-supportive teaching methods are that they

- recognize students' strengths and abilities rather than limitations;

- promote students' volitional actions and perceptions of choice rather than dependency and pressure;

- harness the power of students' passions and curiosity rather than conformity and standardization;

- facilitate students' agency and ownership over learning rather than compliance and obedience; and

- create value through meaningfulness and purpose rather than grades and tests. (Wehmeyer & Zhao, 2020, p. 49)

These teaching methods will hopefully invite and encourage students to take initiative in learning by making learning meaningful and personal. They should also encourage students to act volitionally to make meaningful choices. Self-determined learning involves three basic steps (Wehmeyer & Zhao, 2020, p. 51):

1. Learners self-initiate action to set a goal and achieve a preferred outcome when that outcome aligns with self-interest and is congruent with their passions.

2. Learners self-regulate planning, to create an action plan to address the goal and design a means of measuring their own progress toward the goal.

3. Learners use information they have gathered to evaluate their own progress and adjust their plan or goal, if necessary.

There are specific sets of skills that teachers can use to improve students' ability to exercise self-determination. Self-determination allows students to become causal agents, taking volitional and agentic actions in their life. For example, "To act volitionally, students must use skills that enable them to initiate and engage in *causal* action, including problem-solving, decision-making, goal setting, and planning skills" (Wehmeyer & Zhao, 2020, p. 94).

Problem-solving is essential for students to engage in self-determined learning. Teachers can teach students problem-solving skills such as problem identification, problem definition and formation, generation of alternative solutions, decision-making, and solution implementation. Decision-making is also essential for self-determination. Teachers can teach students skills for decision-making, such as recognizing circumstances leading to the need for a decision, awareness of the need for a decision, identifying the goals of the decision, identifying possible actions, determining consequences of each action, determining probability of each consequence, establishing relative importance of each action and consequence, and integrating the probability and importance to identify the best course of action.

Setting goals is another action that students can learn to boost their self-determination and be more purposeful in their learning. Teachers can teach students the four essential steps in goal-setting: (1) identifying and enunciating goals, (2) developing objectives to meet goals, (3) identifying actions necessary to achieve goals, and (4) tracking and following progress toward goals.

Setting goals is closely linked to planning, a future-focused and goal-oriented process. Planning is the specific process through which goals are realized. For example, while it is good to have the goal of learning something, it is better to also have a plan to achieve that goal because it improves the probability of doing so. Planning is also deeply connected to self-initiation and autonomy. Teachers can help students improve their planning skills by teaching them "pathways thinking" that involves multiple steps (Wehmeyer & Zhao, 2020):

1. Identifying the goal for the planning

2. Breaking the goal down into objectives or steps along the way

3. Identifying different ways of achieving the goal and objectives

4. Choosing the best option, determining resources for implementing the plan

5. Creating timelines

6. Creating evaluations and tracking process

7. Evaluating whether the path is right or whether another path is needed

Agentic engagement is the students' contribution to the instruction they receive. Students can respond to the instructor, ask questions, and engage in the learning process autonomously. Agentic actions require skills that enable students to direct and sustain actions toward agentic engagement. These include skills for self-regulation, such as self-assessment, self-instruction, and self-monitoring, to manage and organize their resources to reach their goals. These skills also involve goal-attainment skills required to sustain action toward a goal.

Finally, it is important to teach students to advocate for themselves and others. Advocacy requires students to be committed to not only what they advocate, but also skills that can help them bring the issues forward. Teachers can help students develop advocacy skills in many ways, including providing experiences related to leadership and teamwork, teaching human rights and other legal rights, teaching assertiveness, and teaching public speaking skills and use of community resources (Wehmeyer & Zhao, 2020).

CULTIVATING FUTURE CREATORS

There is another big question related to having students take charge of their own learning. We know that children are natural-born learners, they are diverse learners, and they desire self-determination. We can also teach them to regain self-determination. The question is, then, what they should learn?

Teachers, school leaders, parents, and policy makers understand and accept that all children are natural-born and diverse learners. They also acknowledge that children should have the right to self-determination and children should be the owners of their learning. But they worry about the future of children. If we allow children to learn what they want to learn, encourage them to act following their own passions, and enable them to become self-determined learners, how can we make sure what they learn will be of value in the future?

This question cannot be easily answered. In fact, no one can predict with great certainty what will be of value in the future, as the future is unpredictable. Unlike a hundred years ago, when societal changes happened much more slowly and industries remained relatively stable for long periods, today industries are drastically redefined in a matter of a few years and jobs change on a large scale very rapidly.

What we can do is prepare students as creators of the future. Instead of trying to predict the future, we should assume that the future is not predetermined—rather, it is fluid. Our students participate in making that future, together with everyone else. Each and every one of our students participates in changing the world in the future. They are not only recipients of changes, but also change makers.

When students are treated as change makers, what they need to know and be able to do in order to thrive is not what is prescribed according to a presumed future. Instead, they need to be themselves, which means they need to sustain their natural passion for learning. Lifelong learning has been advocated for a long time now in education, but rarely do schools teach students to be lifelong learners. Lifelong learning first requires all learners to become owners of their learning, so that they can manage and pursue their learning without the necessity of being pushed by external forces. Lifelong learning also requires learners to know and be able to tackle problems on their own, without being told to do so.

Lifelong learning is also a process of encountering and solving unknown and unpredictable problems continuously. Uncertainty is, perhaps, one of the only situations we can count on in the future. As natural-born learners, students will have to create innovative solutions to unknown problems they encounter instead of simply memorizing existing solutions to known problems, as has been traditionally taught. Teaching students skills in self-determination, such as problem-solving, is of tremendous value for developing skills to create the future.

Moreover, as change makers, not only do students need to have the skills to solve unknown and uncertain problems; they must also have the mindset to take action. This mindset is the instinctual need to explore and learn. It is the desire for autonomy, competence, and relatedness. Only when they can completely and competently exercise autonomy, develop competence, and cultivate relatedness can students become self-determined. This mindset can be called the "entrepreneurial spirit" or "entrepreneurial mindset" (see Zhao, 2012).

ADVOCACY

What schools can do and should do is follow students' human nature, treat their natural tendencies with respect, and support the cultivation of self-determination. Nowhere is this better seen than in student advocacy, both for themselves and for others.

Kanoa, the student from Mid-Pacific Institute, is absolutely right. Students play a significant role in securing their right to self-determination. Self-advocacy is the ultimate factor of self-determination. After all, it is the *self* in "self-determination" that matters. If students are not interested in maintaining ownership of their learning or incapable of managing their own learning, self-determination is but an empty concept. Students must know that formal education is developed to help them advance. They go to school to learn for themselves. Schools are built for students!

Self-advocacy, however, is not sufficient for all students, as another student, Emanuelle, said (Yong Zhao, 2020). Because of the shortcomings of formal education today, many students may have lost the intention or ability to advocate for their own learning. It is also possible that even if they advocate, the school may not respond positively. In some cases, self-advocacy may be considered disruptive to traditional teaching or school rules.

Students may also move past the skills of self-advocacy to advocating on behalf of others. They ought to take action to fight for the less capable and less fortunate. When they advocate for their own learning, they should also advocate for other students who are still learning or unable to advocate for themselves. They should advocate for school-wide changes to enable students to exercise their right to self-determination. In other words, advocacy is for both self and everyone!

SUMMARY

Although the idea that all children are natural-born learners is widely accepted, we do not necessarily respect the idea in our schools. We tend to force children to learn, to trick them with motivational strategies, and to coerce them into learning. This is unnecessary. If we change our educational paradigm to follow human nature, to respect children's talents and interests, children's natural tendency to learn will drive them to learn in school.

This change is difficult but necessary. The task, for educators, is to look at the child rather than look at the curriculum; to believe that the development of the whole child is much more important than forcing everyone to master what has been determined by governments in the curriculum standards; and to give students sufficient time and space to learn to exercise their right to self-determination, so that they can be responsible for their own learning.

CHAPTER 8

Making the Change
Learners Without Borders

W e have arrived at a time when big changes must happen in education, when today's learners are able to break away from the traditional borders imposed upon them. They should not be constrained by schooling, curriculum, and classrooms, nor should they be bounded by assessments and credentialing. This change is not going to be easy, so let us look at some small, evolutionary steps that schools can take to make big changes in the right direction.

ADVOCATING FOR THE RIGHT OUTCOMES

To start considering the changes we need to make in schools, first we need to think about educational outcomes. That is, what should students know and be able to do? Schools are built to help students learn the knowledge and skills needed after they graduate, and schools and teachers are held accountable for ensuring that their students do indeed learn the knowledge and skills. International and national assessments have been developed and deployed to assess to what degree students have mastered the skills and knowledge.

However, several issues related to outcomes need to be examined carefully. We seem to have expected too much of students. In any curriculum, there are school subjects that include literacy, numeracy, sciences, arts, music, physical education, social studies, history, geography, and a host of others. Beyond the specific knowledge subjects, there are expectations of capabilities such as creativity, curiosity, entrepreneurial thinking, critical thinking, collaboration, growth mindset, and resilience. New content and subjects are also being added to the curriculum. Recent years have seen the addition of financial literacy, global competence, and computer coding, among others. Although standardized tests for accountability typically focus on literacy, numeracy, and perhaps science, schools have to deliver a whole range of courses to cover all required outcomes, as well as ways to teach students other capabilities.

The intention is good, as it is schools' and the system's responsibility to help students develop the capabilities to thrive after graduation. We want our children to learn everything that we think is valuable, and we believe that if we try hard, our students can learn everything we want them to learn. Unfortunately, this is not necessarily the case.

I wrote much about the issues with educational outcomes in *What Works May Hurt: Side Effects in Education* (Zhao, 2018e). The primary issue is that different educational outcomes do not necessarily support each other. In fact, they sometimes contradict each other. Because of the conflicting relationship among different educational outcomes, what works to help one outcome can have adverse side effects on other outcomes, similar to how a medication always has potential side effects.

First, there are conflicts among the subjects. That is, if a student pursues one subject, time spent on other subjects is reduced. Time is a constant; every student has only so much time in school. When a student spends time on math, he or she cannot spend that time on sciences. As a result, when schools try to teach too many subjects, it is very likely that the students are unable to explore anything deeply. Some subjects are unavoidably sacrificed. It is not surprising that most students have been studying what has been tested because schools and teachers focus on delivering the tested subjects and content. The many subjects, in the end, turn out to be the few subjects that have been tested.

Second, there are conflicts between cognitive and noncognitive skills. In recent years, attention to people's social and emotional well-being has risen. We want students to be able to perform cognitive tasks, and we also want them to live a happy life. We do not want our students to learn with tremendous anxiety, worry, and distress. We want them to be confident and curious and to love learning. However, data suggests that these outcomes do not necessarily go together. For example, the Programme for International Student Assessment (PISA) found a significant negative correlation between test results and life satisfaction. That is, educational systems that produce high-scoring students seem to produce students who are less satisfied with their life. This is especially true in East Asian educational systems, which have consistently performed extremely well in test scores but have had consistently low levels of life satisfaction. Students in East Asian countries also have had low confidence, and they value less the subjects they perform well on (Zhao, 2018e, 2020d).

Third, outcomes can be long-term or short-term, and they don't always go together. For example, direct instruction can result in shorter-lived learning gains than inquiry-based learning. It seems quite efficient and effective at imparting specific knowledge or teaching students how to perform certain tasks, but this gain may be "unproductive" in the long term because it does not ultimately result in the transfer of knowledge, which means applying the knowledge in different contexts and developing new solutions. Inquiry-based learning may take longer than direct instruction to achieve the short-term outcome, but it can result in a better long-term outcome—the transfer of knowledge (Zhao, 2018e). Furthermore, direct instruction could diminish students' curiosity (Zhao, 2018e).

Unfortunately, most assessment of students' learning in school is about short-term outcomes. Teachers are responsible for teaching certain content and skills in a course. They typically plan their lessons based on a certain period of time or a number of class sessions. Each class session has to be responsible for teaching a certain amount of content/skills, and assessment is given at the end of a class period or multiple periods. There is often also midterm assessment and end-of-the-course assessment. What is assessed is, at the most, one semester of learning and, typically, only the cognitive aspect of learning. Very rarely are students assessed in the areas of knowledge transfer, curiosity, creativity, and other sorts of capabilities.

Given the conflicts about educational outcomes, we as educators need to consider what outcomes are worth promoting. Because, most often, measured outcomes are short-term outcomes, we have a tendency to focus on the "unproductive successes." The outcomes may look great in the short term, but, in the long run, they are meaningless. How much does anyone remember the specific knowledge that we learned in third grade?

The long-term outcomes, especially those noncognitive ones, have usually been ignored in education. These outcomes accompany a person for life and always play a significant role in lifelong learning. Such outcomes include a diversity of human attributes. They can be attitudinal, intentional, mindset, and social-psychological. They go by many names, such as "curiosity," "persistence," "growth mindset," "creativity," "critical thinking," "collaboration," "entrepreneurial mindset," and "communication" (Duckworth & Yeager, 2015; Zhao, Wehmeyer, et al., 2019). They include attributes aligned with specific tasks or subjects, such as whether people are interested in doing something, whether they value certain subjects, or whether they would be passionate about certain jobs. These long-term outcomes are much more important and should be valued more highly than short-term outcomes.

It is worth noting that the human attributes outcomes, the long-term educational outcomes, can be in conflict with each other as well. We can perhaps help each and every student to achieve certain levels of competence in all these areas, but it is difficult to expect everyone to have the same high level of competence in all areas. For example, we can perhaps expect that all students will develop competence in critical thinking, collaboration, communication, and creativity. But it would not be possible for all students to be equally high in all these areas at the highest level, because these qualities do not necessarily support each other. A person can be extremely creative but just a mediocre collaborator. Likewise, another person can be very adept at communication but not so good at critical thinking.

To address these issues, we can apply the idea of *jagged profiles* (Rose, 2016). We should not expect everyone to have the same average abilities. Instead, we should expect individuals to have different proficiencies in different areas. Every individual is likely to be very strong in some areas but very weak in others. As a result, the idea of helping all students develop a unique jagged profile of knowledge, skills, and attributes becomes extremely important. As discussed earlier, governments and schools can and should expect all students to learn the same knowledge and skills at a certain level, so that all can function as civil citizens of the society. But what will help students thrive in the future is their unique strengths and passions.

> What will help students thrive in the future is their unique strengths and passions.

To advocate for unique individuals and make efforts to help each and every student achieve uniqueness and greatness is to let students break out of the traditional boundaries of education. It is to enable students to have a personalized curriculum. It is to facilitate learning using resources outside of the classroom. It is to encourage students to become owners of their learning. It is to ensure that students have the skills and opportunities to become self-determined.

MAKING THE CHANGES

For students to own their learning and break away from the borders of schooling, schools must make several changes. These changes will not happen quickly because we cannot assume that students, parents, teachers, and the public are ready to make big and complex changes overnight. What we need are evolutionary changes that will gradually become a revolution.

The changes schools can make can start with students, teachers, the curriculum, pedagogy, or any angle that the school finds meaningful. There is no particular element that a school should start with, as long as the goal is to liberate students from the borders that constrain their learning. Whichever element a school chooses to focus on first, it is not in the best interest of the school to completely overhaul every element of the school.

While many books on education present specific ideas for how to conduct change, it is my belief that any changes should come from the teachers, principals, students, and parents. All changes have to be meaningful to the local contexts, and it is the local actors who can come up with great solutions. In this book, it is not my intention to offer details of *how* to enact changes. Rather, I offer the arguments and general principles for such changes. Let us now explore some avenues that schools and teachers can take to make the changes.

Underserved Students

Schools, no matter how good they are, typically do not serve all students equally well. There is no one educational approach that meets the needs of all students and teaches everything right all the time (Zhao, 2017, 2018e). There is always a group of students who are not served well by a school or class. These students may be unable to stay engaged in what is offered in the school. They may also not be able to keep up with the demands of the classes. They may not have been able to find anything the school offers interesting. Or they may just be interested in learning or doing something different. Whatever the reason, in every school, the bottom quartile of students are behind the school's expectations. That's a lot.

These students need changes. We should not view them as less capable or simply slower than other students. These students may have great talents in areas other than the school curriculum but no opportunity to express those talents. It is also possible that these students possess a background that disadvantages them. Furthermore, it is possible that these students are looking for new ways of teaching and learning. If the students are not responding to what is offered to them, it is important that schools develop and offer new possibilities rather than the traditional remediation courses they typically receive.

The new possibilities start with personalization. A school could offer a new program to focus on providing personalized education (Zhao, 2018b, 2018c). The program does not have to be run by many teachers. It could start with one teacher, but the teacher is not there to teach. The teacher's primary responsibility is to work with these students on personalizing their learning pathways. The teacher would start by promoting and recruiting students into the program, making it clear that this program allows students to learn what they want to learn, primarily on their own with the support of teachers. The teacher would then work with each student to discover that student's interests and strengths and develop a learning plan in collaboration with his or her parents or guardians. Afterward, the teacher's job is to go through the process of learning with students and constantly examine and revise the personalized learning plans.

Entrepreneurial Students

In Chapter 4, we considered a special population of students who often struggle with schooling: young entrepreneurs. These students have found what they can do and are interested in, but what they do as entrepreneurs has little to do with what they do in school. So they have to manage both jobs, so to speak.

As entrepreneurship becomes more important in society and many more youths have expressed interest in pursuing entrepreneurship, schools need to find a way to accommodate and help these students. Although some schools have begun to offer entrepreneurship courses or after-school clubs, these are not sufficient to help these students. First, the entrepreneurship courses are typically not part of the mainstream curriculum. They can be meaningful to inspire students' entrepreneurship interests and teach them some basic skills, but they are not meant to support students' continuous efforts in running businesses. Second, the courses are typically short, lasting perhaps one semester or a year, but students' entrepreneurship activities can become very real and keep going for years. Even if an entrepreneurship course is meaningful, it does not last long enough to be of value to the students. Third, the content of many entrepreneurship courses is hypothetical, rarely involving having students operate real businesses. But the young entrepreneurs are engaged in real businesses and thus have different needs for knowledge and skills.

The total number of young entrepreneurs in school is still small, but it can grow quickly if schools find ways to support them. This is also a group of students who have a strong desire to seek and realize self-determination but currently have little school support. Schools could start making changes in favor of young entrepreneurs in several ways.

Schools could, at least, consider what young entrepreneurs do as learning experiences and count their experiences as part of the required curriculum. This would legitimize entrepreneurship as a process of learning, and, indeed, students are learning a lot from their entrepreneurship activities. And it would be productive for schools to develop a program, not just a course, for young entrepreneurs. The program's focus should be personalized learning, with an emphasis on entrepreneurship. This would stimulate more entrepreneurship among students and provide a community for young entrepreneurs. Finally, schools might work with each and every young entrepreneur to completely personalize their learning, so that their entrepreneurship activities are enhanced as a result of their learning and so that such learning is part of their required learning.

Unique Students

Besides youth entrepreneurs, there are other students with unusual talents and passions. Their talents and passions may not be entrepreneurship, nor are they deeply connected to school subjects. Instead, their passions may be what drove Greta Thunberg to start protesting on climate issues. Or their talents may be in writing novels, learning about astrophysics, working on taking care of animals, music, art, or dancing.

Many of these students cannot find a place in traditional schooling to develop or demonstrate their talents and passions. This can result in their losing interest and engagement in school, even giving up their talents and interests. What a loss for all of us.

Schools can work with these students to create opportunities for them to learn beyond the strictures of the curriculum and beyond the classroom. Students with different interests and talents can be guided to find learning resources online and in the community. They can work on passion projects. Schools, again, can organize a special program for these students.

Working with students who are not benefiting from the existing offerings or who have other passions and talents is a fairly easy step to introduce some of the changes discussed in this book. The overall approach is to create alternative pathways for students. Quite often, many students are prepared and have been waiting for such opportunities. The school does not need to make sure that everything is ready. We need to believe in students' desire for self-determination and their natural aptitude for learning. What schools need to do is to recognize and acknowledge that students have different talents and passions that require space to be developed and demonstrated.

Passion Projects and Genius Hours

Schools can also start by making small changes to the time students spend in school. In many schools, all time has been divided into class periods and all class periods have been assigned to certain subjects. There is little free time for students to explore their own interests. This follows the traditional grammar of schooling. Parents love it because they feel their children are being taught all the time. Schools have been used to this grammar for generations.

But, as has been discussed in this book, students should have their own time to study their own personal curriculum. If a student's curriculum is made of three parts—government-mandated, school-mandated, and personal—he or she needs to have time to work on his or her own learning. A school may not be able to devote too much time to personal learning in the beginning, but it can give every student a taste of such independent learning by offering *passion projects* or *genius hours*.

Passion projects can be done in individual classrooms or across the entire school. The formula is fairly simple—students just need an allotted time to follow their passion and explore, carry out, and complete a project. In the beginning, a teacher can do what Chris Aviles, a teacher in New Jersey, did with his students: allow the students to do whatever they like for an English class and come back to report what they did at the end of semester (Zhao, 2018c).

One way of elevating passion projects to an institution is to implement genius hours. The idea of genius hours came from the tech giant Google, which allocates about 20 percent of work time for employees to work on something they are interested in. Google has found that such an arrangement enhanced workers' productivity and resulted in unexpected and popular products, such as Gmail and Google News. Educators have taken the idea into schools. They can allow about 20 percent of time in school or in class for students to pursue their own interests and work on projects they are passionate about.

Passion projects and genius hours are essentially the same thing. They give students autonomy, which is an essential part of self-determination. When students have autonomy, they are able to enjoy the right to self-determination. Thus, they can freely exercise their own interests and build on their strengths.

Electives and Courses by Students

Another approach that schools can take is to increase the number of elective courses available. Electives, or optional courses, have existed in schools, particularly high schools, for a long time. But the number and content have been limited. Given the goal of enabling students to take control of their own learning, it is advisable for schools to drastically expand their offerings. Besides encouraging teachers to offer more diverse courses, schools can work with other schools to increase their course offerings. For example, the Global Online Academy, a consortium of schools from different continents, has been supporting teachers to provide courses for students in consortium-wide schools. Schools can also bring in other online courses by collaborating with communities and organizations such as MOOC operators, nonprofits, and universities.

A very important way to increase the number of elective courses is to invite students in the school to offer courses they may be interested in. As we know, students are quite capable and have different talents and passions. We also know that students can learn tremendously by teaching and tutoring others, so it would be productive to have students provide elective courses or tutoring sessions to their fellow students. These courses can be solicited from students and be reviewed by a curriculum committee composed of teachers and students. They could also undergo serious evaluations at the conclusion of the course. In addition, teachers and students can work together on offering these courses as a team.

Teacher Initiatives

Schools should also encourage and support teachers to be innovative. One of the things schools can do to help teachers become more innovative is to humanize teaching so that instruction encompasses the education of the entire child rather than simply emphasizing the course content. Teachers have interests and passions and should have an opportunity to exercise their own self-determination for the purpose of education. Thus, schools can invite teachers to offer elective courses that match their talents and passions. Schools can also encourage teachers to infuse themselves into the traditional courses they teach.

> To humanize teaching is to treat teaching as the education of the entire child rather than simply emphasizing the course content.

But the most important change for teachers is for them to use technology. They can use technology to replace their instruction, to take care of grades and homework, and to bring in outside experts. Allowing technology to siphon off the tasks that human beings are not good at, not interested in, or not capable of doing releases teachers from the necessity of being instructional machines. They can then become human educators. Human educators see their students as fellow human beings; they work with students to develop their humanity and help them reach their greatest potential; they see students first and the curriculum second.

When teachers are able to relieve themselves of the traditional, boring, and mechanical aspects of their work, they are invited to develop new initiatives for students. Teachers can establish alternative programs for students who are not engaged in the traditional teaching. They can allow students in their classes to learn different things from what they teach. They are able to support students' projects outside their classes. They can also be managing new programs the school decides to offer for students who are seeking different pathways of learning.

Student-Led Initiatives

Schools can make changes by encouraging and accepting student-led initiatives. There are some students who are not happy with their school's offerings and are interested in developing their own programs. For example, Sam Levin, a Massachusetts high-school student, proposed the Independent Project, essentially a school for those interested in pursuing their own learning. He and other students made a plan of learning and got the high school's support. They ran the program for a semester and saw very positive results (Levin & Engel, 2016).

Perhaps not many students have the courage to start their own school, as Sam Levin did. But it is not impossible, especially when schools openly encourage such actions. Moreover, teachers and school leaders can create mechanisms to inspire students to create their own schools or programs, as well as provide support for such initiatives.

School Within a School

A school within a school is an excellent model for introducing the entire new paradigm of education to some students. It is unwise for a school to overhaul itself all at once, but it is feasible and productive to create new options. In any school, there are diverse students and parents who have different views of education. These students and parents may have no choice in schools and have to be there, which is the case in many public schools. Even in private schools, where students and parents choose to be, there is still sufficient diversity and expectations, as discussed earlier in the book. One of the problems that schools have with a diverse population and parents is that they typically offer one model of education, as discussed earlier. Students and parents have to live with what they have.

Increasing options in schools is a productive measure that will not alienate those students, parents, and teachers who love the traditional approach of education while attracting those students, parents, and teachers who are not big fans of the traditional approach. Adding a new school that is completely different from, but still within, the traditional school will make it possible for students and staff to follow a new educational paradigm.

The new school exists in the old one but should operate independently of the traditional curriculum and teaching. The new school supports students as co-owners of the school. Each and every student has their own curriculum—part government-mandated, part school-mandated, and part personal curriculum. The students are not organized in the traditional way, to be taught by one instructor in one class. Instead, they choose to take different courses from school offerings and take courses online from other providers. They can also learn from local communities and other students. They work with individual teachers, who serve as consultants and resources for students. Their learning is driven by creating solutions to meaningful problems they identify. They enjoy autonomy, competence, and relatedness in the school.

The students are also co-owners of their school environments. They work together, with teachers, to decide the various aspects of the school's operations. Together they decide the social infrastructure of their school, which includes rules and regulations that govern their behaviors and activities. They also decide the intellectual infrastructure, which includes the intellectual content and staff, of the school. They can decide what courses should be offered and what staff they want to work with. They can also decide how to make use of their physical environments, such as libraries and classes, in addition to purchases of technological equipment and books (Zhao, 2012, 2018c).

The new school should be open to all students who are interested in this new approach. Marketing this new school is critical. Students and parents must receive enough information and have enough conversations with the new school staff and leaders to get a clear sense of the school's mission and operations. They must know that the students are the owners of their own learning and, thus, must be willing to take up this responsibility. They must also understand that the school's success is dependent on both students and staff.

The "school within a school" model aims to plant a seed of big changes for the future. Its operations can and should be very visible to other students and staff, so that others can perceive and understand the new learning possibilities. The school should regularly hold public exhibitions, to expose outsiders to students' work products. The school can also have open days, for others to visit the school and talk with staff and students. The overall idea is to provide exposure for the new school as much as possible, in the hope that others will find it interesting and decide to join.

LEARNERS WITHOUT BORDERS

"Learners without borders" is my dream for education. There are many factors working against the dream. Chief among them are cultural and historical traditions. We have had many brave and courageous people trying to change the "grammar of schooling" for over a century, but the basic structure of schools remains the same (Tyack & Cuban, 1995; Tyack & Tobin, 1994).

Today, the difficulty in changing how schools operate remains. But now even more people are working on new models of learning, technologies have further advanced, and globalization has increased. More important, we know more about how human brains work than ever before, educators are connected to one another around the world, and there is mounting evidence that the traditional educational model does not work for all students. We also know that the world demands new talents, and we have a lot more active youths. Moreover, COVID-19 has expanded our notions of how education can be offered, and it has stimulated massive innovations (Zhao, 2020a, 2020c).

A Global Learning Ecosystem

The new education would enable learners to learn without borders. Learning happens in a global learning ecosystem. Within this ecosystem are numerous learning opportunities, both remote and local. These opportunities for learning are created by the learner and by teachers with learning resources. For example, a student can be learning from virtual museums or remote scientific tools. The student can also be interacting with students in other lands. The student can also be participating in online conferences or meetings.

The global learning ecosystem includes schools and other groups of students around the world. Schools, or other forms of organization of students, are where students spend most of their time and are primarily accounted for. Each school, however, can be connected with other schools and organizations. Students, thus, can participate in learning offered by different schools. Their learning need not be limited to the local school they are enrolled in.

The global learning ecosystem provides unlimited niches for different talents. Given the diversity of students' strengths and passions, no one school can truly meet the needs of all students. Thus, to enable students to develop their passions and strengths, we need a global learning ecosystem that includes learning opportunities from afar and local. This ecosystem can include opportunities for mentorship, internship, camps, classes, meetings, projects, and other forms of learning. The opportunities are very diverse and provided by many thousands of organizations in different parts of the world.

The global learning ecosystem can be organized by schools, but it is largely realized by each and every learner, who are not confined by the borders of schooling. When students are self-determined learners, they should have the right and ability to learn globally. They should be able to work with their teachers to reach out to institutions and individuals around the globe. They should be able to participate in massive learning environments such as Scratch (Resnick, 2017a) and fanfiction sites (Aragon & Davis, 2019). They should be able to have access to and learn from MOOCs (Bonk et al., 2015).

The Brave Learners

The learning ecosystem, in essence, already exists, but whether it is activated depends largely on the learner. Almost ten years ago, I received a phone call from Nikhil Goyal, a student in high school. He told me that he was interested in writing a book about education and he would like to interview me. I was very surprised that a high-school student wanted to write a book on education, but I gladly accepted the interview request. I think I learned a lot more from Nikhil than he did from me. It was apparent that he had been talking to a lot of educators and that he took on the task of learning about education because he was not happy with it. Later, I met him on a stage with a number of well-known speakers in the field of education. I learned that he had had to find ways to leave high school in order to travel to speak. His book *One Size Does Not Fit All: A Student's Assessment of School* (Goyal, 2012) has received praise from former U.S. assistant secretary of education Diane Ravitch and Harvard professor of cognition and education Howard Gardner.

Nikhil constructed and utilized his global learning ecosystem. He is a learner without borders. His book was not a school project or part of the school curriculum. He was not bound by his school, his curriculum, or his teachers. He told me that his school did not know what he was doing. Neither did his teachers. He reached out to anyone he considered valuable for his learning, wherever they were. Nikhil, by the way, has continued his interest in education and completed another book on education: *Schools on Trial: How Freedom and Creativity Can Fix Our Educational Malpractice* (Goyal, 2016).

He is currently completing his doctorate in sociology at Cambridge University with a focus on inequity in education.

Many other brave students have dived into the global learning ecosystem without borders. As mentioned in Chapter 4, Greta Thunberg is someone whose learning journey has changed because of her brave actions outside the Swedish parliament at the age of fifteen. She now travels and speaks in public and in private, convincing others of the tough issues we must all face due to climate change. She learns as well. She has certainly expanded her own learning through her interactions with others. Sam Levin, the student who started a school within a school, is another example of someone breaking the borders of schooling.

The Unknown and Uncertain

Learners without borders are students who are not only interested in learning beyond the confinement of their school and curriculum, but also comfortable with and interested in exploring the unknown and uncertain. Following the predetermined curriculum, attending classes, listening to teachers, completing homework, and taking exams may be hard, but they are all known and certain. If a student does all that is asked of him or her in school, the work is hard but not challenging. One of the biggest problems with current schooling is the lack of opportunities for students to be engaged in dealing with uncertainties and unknowns, according to professor of educational psychology Ron Beghetto, whom I mentioned in Chapter 2. Ron told me in my interview with him that what schools teach is typically known solutions to known problems. Very rarely does school learning involve the unknown and uncertain (Beghetto, 2018a, 2018b).

But the future is filled with unknowns and uncertainties. The acronym VUCA, for volatile, uncertain, complex, and ambiguous, describes the future and the world that confronts us (Carvan, 2015). There is no question that our students will be in ample VUCA situations after they graduate from school. There is, thus, no reason to protect them and pretend that VUCA challenges do not exist. Instead, we should work on exposing them to and having them address VUCA situations while they are in school.

The global learning ecosystem can be an excellent context for students to be engaged with VUCA problems. When students go beyond their school's confines, they are most likely engaged in learning beyond their traditional classroom offerings, exploring something authentic and meaningful.

The 3M Young Scientist Lab (Discovery Education, 2020b) is a great example of students engaged beyond their schoolwork. The lab runs an annual competition for middle-school students. Reading materials for some of the 2020 winners suggest that these students have gone way beyond their middle-school science classes. They have tackled significant real problems and proposed innovative solutions. They have learned way outside of their classrooms. The internet has helped them tremendously. One of the winners, Anika Chebrolu, a student from Texas, highlighted the Internet as her favorite invention of the last hundred years:

> My favorite invention is the Internet because it allows us to explore so much with just a few clicks. I find it a treasure trove of information and it has become a valuable asset in pursuing knowledge and conducting research from anywhere and at anytime. I am amazed at how vast and profound it is and cannot imagine a world without the internet. When coupled with proper judgement and use, we can achieve so much more and I am enthused at its potential each time I use it. (quoted in Discovery Education, 2020a)

Blended Learning

The Internet is the backbone of the global learning ecosystem. Students who wish to break out of the borders of schooling must use the Internet to connect to others. They must also rely on technology to have access to resources beyond their school. The Internet and related technologies are the tools for students to participate in the global learning ecosystem.

Blended learning, or hybrid learning (C. R. Tucker, 2020), has been advocated and promoted. Teachers have been encouraged to use technology to bring external learning materials and experts into their classrooms. COVID-19 has made remote learning a universal experience for students and teachers around the world.

The remote learning experiences can be a catalyst for developing blended learning experiences once students are back in school. It would be a shame to see schools drop remote learning in favor of a complete return to in-person learning.

Successful blended learning requires autonomy and self-determination on the part of students. This is what I learned from Catlin Tucker, a teacher and author of *Balance With Blended Learning: Partner With Your Students to Reimagine Learning and Reclaim Your Life* (C. R. Tucker, 2020). Catlin told me that blended learning is an approach that can help teachers relax and give the class to students. The ultimate goal is to give students the autonomy and space for their own learning.

CONCLUSION: CAN CHANGE HAPPEN?

Before I started writing this book, I interviewed many experts in education. I asked all of them to comment on the current state of education and educational innovations. (You can view the interviews by going to http://bit.ly/learnerswithoutborders). I was quite struck by the general message that, although for a long time we have had many innovations in education, innovations are not in use in more than 10 percent of schools.

This message was what I got from my interviews with Ted Dintersmith and Dr. Milton Chen. Milton told me about proposed big changes in education over the past fifty years but said that not many schools are engaged with the changes.

But the message is not that education *cannot* change, because everyone I interviewed is actively engaged in promoting changes in education—through presentations, professional development offerings, books, and educational programs.

Luba Vangelova is a parent and an education entrepreneur who has been active in seeking new ways of educating children. Recently she has focused on the innovations that parents are seeking and developing outside of schools. COVID-19 has definitely accelerated the pace of innovation among parents, who are eager to find new possibilities for their children. In 2020, Luba launched *The Hub* (The Hub.Community, 2020), an online learning program for children: "The Hub's mission is to help independent life-long learners have the best of both worlds: customization and community" (The Hub.Community, 2020).

Besides these people I have interviewed, I have also seen a large number of researchers, teachers, school leaders, students, and parents engage in advocating, promoting, asking for, and making changes in education. A primary goal of these changes is to liberate students from traditional schooling. It is, indeed, true that the majority of schools are not actively making big changes, but some are changing. We cannot expect governments and educational systems to lead the big changes we need.

However, the time has arrived. We can and should let students become learners without borders!

References

Akçayır, G., & Akçayır, M. (2018). The flipped classroom: A review of its advantages and challenges. *Computers & Education, 126,* 334–345.

Alter, C., Haynes, S., & Worland, J. (2020). *Time* 2019 Person of the Year: Greta Thunberg. *Time.* https://time.com/person-of-the-year-2019-greta-thunberg

American Psychological Association. (2012). *Facing the school dropout dilemma.* http://www.apa.org/pi/families/resources/school-dropout-prevention.aspx

Aragon, C. R., & Davis, K. (2019). *Writers in the secret garden: Fanfiction, youth, and new forms of mentoring.* MIT Press.

Associated Press. (1923, May 15). Edison predicts film will replace teacher, books. *Highland Recorder, 45*(20), 2. https://virginiachronicle.com/cgi-bin/virginia?a=d&d=HR1923 0518.2.11&e=-------en-20--1--txt-txIN--------

Barber, M., Donnelly, K., & Rizvi, S. (2012). *Oceans of innovation: The Atlantic, the Pacific, global leadership and the future of education.* Institute for Public Policy Research. https://www.ippr.org/publications/oceans-of-innovation-the-atlantic-the-pacific-global-leadership-and-the-future-of-education

Barnum, M. (2020, October 6). How much learning have students lost due to COVID? Projections are coming in, but it's still hard to say. *Chalkbeat.* https://www.chalkbeat.org/2020/10/6/21504195/covid-schools-learning-loss-projections-nwea-credo

BBC News. (2019, December 30). *Surge in teenagers setting up businesses, study suggests.* https://www.bbc.com/news/newsbeat-50938854

Beard, A. (2018). *Natural born learners: Our incredible capacity to learn and how we can harness it*. Hachette UK.

Beghetto, R. A. (2016). *Big wins, small steps: How to lead for and with creativity*. Corwin.

Beghetto, R. (2018a). *Beautiful risks: Having the courage to teach and learn creatively*. Rowman & Littlefield.

Beghetto, R. (2018b). *What if? Building students' problem-solving skills through complex challenges*. ASCD.

Blazar, D., Kane, T. J., Staiger, D., Goldhaber, D., Hitch, R., Kurlaender, M., Heller, B., Polikoff, M., Carrell, S., Harris, D., & Holden, K. L. (2019). *Learning by the book: Comparing math achievement growth by textbook in six common core states*. https://cepr.harvard.edu/files/cepr/files/cepr-curriculum-report_learning-by-the-book.pdf

Bonk, C. J. (2011). *The world is open: How web technology is revolutionizing education*. Jossey-Bass.

Bonk, C. J., Lee, M. M., Reeves, T. C., & Reynolds, T. H. (Eds.). (2015). *MOOCs and open education around the world*. Routledge.

Bohrnstedt, G., Kitmitto, S., Ogut, B., Sherman, D., & Chan, D. (2015, September 24). *School composition and the black–white achievement gap* (NCES 2015-018). National Assessment of Educational Progress. https://nces.ed.gov/nationsreportcard/pubs/studies/2015018.aspx

Bransford, J. D., Brown, A. L., & Cocking, R. R. (Eds.). (2000). *How people learn: Brain, mind, experience, and school*. The National Academies Press.

Buttaro, A., Jr., & Catsambis, S. (2019). Ability grouping in the early grades: Long-term consequences for educational equity in the United States. *Teachers College Record, 121*(2), n2.

Carvan, M. T. (2015). Leadership education for the volatile, uncertain, complex, and ambiguous now: A challenge to the field. *Journal of Leadership Education, 14*(4), 3–10.

Chen, M. (2010). *Education nation: Six leading edges of innovation in our schools*. Jossey-Bass.

Christensen, C. M., Horn, M. B., & Johnson., C. W. (2010). *Disrupting class, expanded edition: How disruptive innovation will change the way the world learns* (2nd ed.). McGraw-Hill.

Clynes, T. (2017, February 22). Peter Thiel thinks you should skip college, and he'll even pay you for your trouble. *Newsweek*

Magazine. https://www.newsweek.com/2017/03/03/peter-thiel-fellowship-college-higher-education-559261.html

Conger, K. (2020, May 21). Facebook starts planning for permanent remote workers. *New York Times.* https://www.nytimes.com/2020/05/21/technology/facebook-remote-work-coronavirus.html

Cuban, L. (1986). *Teachers and machines: The classroom uses of technology since 1920.* Teachers College Press.

Cuban, L. (1993). Computers meet classroom: Classroom wins. *Teachers College Record, 95*(2), 185–210.

Cullen, A. (2019, August 25). *Teen millionaires: The kids running successful businesses who say you can too.* 7 News. https://7news.com.au/sunday-night/teen-millionaires-the-kids-running-successful-businesses-who-say-you-can-too-c-414921

Deci, E. L., & Vansteenkiste, M. (2004). Self-determination theory and basic need satisfaction: Understanding human development in positive psychology. *Ricerche di Psicologia, 27*(1), 23–40.

Dewey, J. (1897). My pedagogic creed. *School Journal, 54,* 77–80.

Dezuanni, M. (2020). *Peer pedagogies on digital platforms: Learning with Minecraft Let's Play Videos.* MIT Press.

Dintersmith, T. (2019). *What school could be: Insights and inspiration from teachers across America.* Princeton University Press.

Discovery Education. (2020a). *Combating the COVID-19 pandemic: In-silico molecular docking study of spike protein of SARS-CoV-2 virus to develop novel antiviral drug.* Young Scientist Lab. https://www.youngscientistlab.com/entry/2397

Discovery Education. (2020b). *Home.* Young Scientist Lab. https://www.youngscientistlab.com

Duckworth, A. L., & Yeager, D. S. (2015). Measurement matters: Assessing personal qualities other than cognitive ability for educational purposes. *Educational Researcher, 44*(4), 237–251.

Elmore, R. (2011, May 18). Opinion: What happens when learning breaks out in rural Mexico? *Education Week.* http://blogs.edweek.org/edweek/futures_of_reform/2011/05/what_happens_when_learning_breaks_out_in_rural_mexico.html

Elmore, R. (2016, January 18). *Reflections on the role of tutoria in the future of learning.* https://redesdetutoria.com/download/69/articulos/11392/reflections-on-role-of-tutoria.pdf

Ervin, B., Sacerdote, C., & Murray, A. K. (2016). *Examining the literature on authentic Montessori practices: Multi-age groupings*. AMS Research Committee White Paper.

Florida, R. (2012). *The rise of the creative class: Revisited* (2nd ed.). Basic Books.

Freeman, R. B. (1980). The facts about the declining economic value of college. *The Journal of Human Resources, 15*(1), 124–142.

Freeman, R., & Hollomon, J. H. (1975). The declining value of college going. *Change: The Magazine of Higher Learning, 7*(7), 24–62.

Fried, I. (2018, November 19). *Tim Cook discusses staying human in an AI world*. Axios. https://www.axios.com/tim-cook-apple-artificial-intelligence-human-ec98a548-0a2f-4a7a-bd65-b4d25395bc27.html

Fried, R. L. (2001). Passionate learners and the challenge of schooling. *Phi Delta Kappan, 83*(2), 124–136.

Gardner, H. (2006). *Multiple intelligences: New horizons* (Rev. and updated ed.). BasicBooks; Perseus Running [distributor].

Gigova, R., & Howard, J. (2020, August 4). *We're facing a 'generational catastrophe' in education, UN warns*. CNN. https://www.cnn.com/2020/08/04/world/school-closures-catastrophe-un-covid-19-intl/index.html

Giroux, H. A., & Penna, A. N. (1979). Social education in the classroom: The dynamics of the hidden curriculum. *Theory & Research in Social Education, 7*(1), 21–42.

Goldin, C., & Katz, L. F. (2008). *The race between education and technology*. Harvard University Press.

Google Career Certificates. (2020). Google Career Certificates. https://grow.google/certificates

Gopnik, A. (2016). *The gardener and the carpenter: What the new science of child development tells us about the relationship between parents and children*. Macmillan.

Gopnik, A., Meltzoff, A. N., & Kuhl, P. K. (1999). *The scientist in the crib: Minds, brains, and how children learn*: William Morrow & Co.

Goyal, N. (2012). *One size does not fit all: A student's assessment of school*. Alternative Education Resource Organization.

Goyal, N. (2016). *Schools on trial: How freedom and creativity can fix our educational malpractice*. Doubleday, an Imprint of Penguin Random House.

Greenberg, D., Sadofsky, M., & Lempka, J. (2005). *The pursuit of happiness: The lives of Sudbury Valley alumni*. Sudbury School Press.

Grenyer, N. (1999). *Summerhill School*. Ofsted. http://www.ofsted.gov.uk/inspection-reports/find-inspection-report/provider/ELS/124870

Grobstein, P., & Lesnick, A. (2011). Education is life itself: Biological evolution as a model for human learning. *Evolution: Education and Outreach, 4*(4), 688–700.

Grundy, S. (1987). *Curriculum: Product or praxis?* Falmer Press.

Hartmans, A. (2020, September 27). Google's CEO says the future of work involves a 'hybrid model' and that the company is already reconfiguring its offices for employee 'on-sites.' *Business Insider*. https://www.businessinsider.com/google-office-future-employee-on-sites-sundar-pichai-2020-9

HundrED.org. (2020). *Redes de Tutoría*. https://hundred.org/en/innovations/redes-de-tutoria

Ireson, J., & Hallam, S. (2001). *Ability grouping in education*. SAGE.

John, O. P., Robins, R. W., & Pervin, L. A. (Eds.). (2008). *Handbook of personality: Theory and research* (3rd ed.). Guilford Press.

Junior Achievement of Greater Washington. (2018, November 6). *National Entrepreneurship Month research shows 41 percent of teens would consider starting a business as a career option* [Press release]. https://www.myja.org/news/latest/2018/11/6/national-entrepreneurship-month-research-shows-41-percent-of-teens-would-consider-starting-a-business-as-a-career-option

Kane, T. J., & Steiner, D. M. (2019, April 1). Don't give up on curriculum reform just yet: What the research does (and doesn't) say about curriculum. *Education Week*. https://www.edweek.org/ew/articles/2019/04/02/dont-give-up-on-curriculum-reform-just.html

Kelly, A. V. (2009). *The curriculum: Theory and practice* (6th ed.). SAGE.

Khan, S. (2012). *The one world schoolhouse: Education reimagined*. Twelve.

Kirp, D. L. (2019, July 30). The college dropout scandal. *Chronicle of Higher Education*. https://www.chronicle.com/article/the-college-dropout-scandal

Knoll, M. (2014). Laboratory School, University of Chicago. In D. C. Phillips (Ed.), *Encyclopedia of Educational Theory and Philosophy* (Vol. 2, pp. 455–458). SAGE.

Lepper, M. P., Greene, D., & Nisbett, R. E. (1973). Undermining children's intrinsic interest with extrinsic reward: A test of the "overjustification" hypothesis. *Journal of Personality and Social Psychology, 28*(1), 129–137. doi:10.1037/h0035519

Levin, S., & Engel, S. (2016). *A school of our own: The story of the first student-run high school and a new vision for American education*. The New Press.

Lewontin, R. (2001). *The triple helix: Gene, organism, and environment*. Harvard University Press.

Marinova, P. (2016, September 15). 18 under 18: Meet the young innovators who are changing the world. *Forbes*. https://fortune .com/2016/09/15/18-entrepreneurs-under-18-teen-business

McQuillan, J. (1996). The effects of incentives on reading. *Reading Research and Instruction, 36*(2), 111–125. doi:10.1080/ 19388079709558232

Mitra, S. (2007, February). *Kids can teach themselves* [Video]. TED Conferences. https://www.ted.com/talks/sugata_mitra_ shows_how_kids_teach_themselves

Mitra, S. (2020). *The school in the cloud: The emerging future of learning*. Corwin.

Mullis, I. V. S., Martin, M. O., & Loveless, T. (2016). *20 Years of TIMSS: International trends in mathematics and science: Achievement, curriculum, and instruction*. International Association for the Evaluation of Educational Achievement. http://timssandpirls.bc.edu/timss2015/international-results/ timss2015/wp-content/uploads/2016/T15-20-years-of- TIMSS.pdf.

Muro, M., Whiton, J., & Maxim, R. (2019, November 20). *What jobs are affected by AI? Better-paid, better-educated workers face the most exposure*. Brookings Institution. https://www .brookings.edu/research/what-jobs-are-affected-by-ai- better-paid-better-educated-workers-face-the-most-exposure

National Academies of Sciences, Engineering, and Medicine. (2018). *How people learn II: Learners, contexts, and cultures*. The National Academies Press.

National Assessment of Educational Progress. (2020a). *NAEP Report Card: 2019 NAEP Mathematics Assessment: Highlighted results at grade 12 for the nation*. https://www.nations- reportcard.gov/highlights

National Assessment of Educational Progress. (2020b). *NAEP Report Card: 2019 NAEP Reading Assessment: Highlighted results at grade 12 for the nation*. https://www.nationsreportcard .gov/highlights/reading/2019/g12

Negroponte, N. P. (1995). *Being digital*. Alfred A Knopf.

Omnicore Agency. (2021, January 6). *YouTube by the numbers: Stats, demographics & fun facts*. https://www.omnicoreagency .com/youtube-statistics

Organisation for Economic Cooperation and Development. (2019). *PISA 2018 results (Volume I): What students know and can do*. OECD Publishing. https://www.oecd-ilibrary .org/education/pisa-2018-results-volume-i_5f07c754-en

Park, V., & Datnow, A. (2017). Ability grouping and differentiated instruction in an era of data-driven decision making. *American Journal of Education, 123*(2), 281–306.

Pink, D. H. (2006). *A whole new mind: Why right-brainers will rule the future*. Riverhead.

Pinsker, J. (2020, February 21). Oh no, they've come up with another generation label. *The Atlantic*. https://www.theatlantic .com/family/archive/2020/02/generation-after-gen-z-named-alpha/606862

ProCon.org. (2020, January 30). *Is a college education worth it?* https://college-education.procon.org

Reiss, S. (2004). Multifaceted nature of intrinsic motivation: The theory of 16 basic desires. *Review of General Psychology, 8*(3), 179–183. https://doi.org/10.1037%2F1089-2680.8.3.179

Reiss, S. (2008). *The normal personality: A new way of thinking about people*. Cambridge University Press.

Resnick, M. (2017). *Lifelong kindergarten: Cultivating creativity through projects, passion, peers, and play*. MIT Press.

Rideout, V., & Robb, M. B. (2019). *The Common Sense census: Media use by tweens and teens, 2019*. Common Sense Media.

Ridley, M. (2003). *Nature via nurture: Genes, experience, and what makes us human*. HarperCollins.

Rose, T. (2016). *The end of average: How we succeed in a world that values sameness*. HarperOne.

Russell, S. (2019, June 16). Schooling v. education. *Age of Awareness*. https://medium.com/age-of-awareness/schooling-v-education-e8ab5ffc4f17

Ryan, R. M., & Deci, E. L. (2017). *Self-determination theory: Basic psychological needs in motivation, development, and wellness*. Guilford Press.

Shafer, S. (2020, August 19). Overcoming COVID-19 learning loss. *Education Week*. https://www.edweek.org/ew/issues/reopening-schools/overcoming-covid-19-learning-loss.html

Shalom, M., & Luria, E. (2019). The multi-age school structure: Its value and contributions in relation to significant learning. *Educational Practice and Theory, 41*(1), 5–21.

Slavin, R. E. (1987). Ability grouping and student achievement in elementary schools: A best-evidence synthesis. *Review of Educational Research, 57*(3), 293–336.

Sleeman, D., & Brown, J. S. (1982). *Intelligent tutoring systems*. Academic Press.

Smilkstein, R. (2011). *We're born to learn: Using the brain's natural learning process to create today's curriculum* (2nd ed.). Corwin.

Smith, M. K. (2000). *What is curriculum? Exploring theory and practice*. The Encyclopedia of Informal Education. https://infed.org/curriculum-theory-and-practice

Sparks, S. D. (2017, September 26). Teachers' jobs aren't going away, but they could be different. *Education Week*. https://www.edweek.org/ew/articles/2017/09/27/how-intelligent-tutors-could-transform-teaching.html

Stanford, P. (2008, January 24). Summerhill: Inside England's most controversial private school. *The Independent*. http://www.independent.co.uk/news/education/schools/summerhill-inside-englands-most-controversial-private-school-772976.html

Statista. (2021a, February 2). *Facebook MAU worldwide 2020*. https://www.statista.com/statistics/264810/number-of-monthly-active-facebook-users-worldwide

Statista. (2021b, February 9). *Most used social media 2020*. https://www.statista.com/statistics/272014/global-social-networks-ranked-by-number-of-users

Steenbergen-Hu, S., Makel, M. C., & Olszewski-Kubilius, P. (2016). What one hundred years of research says about the effects of ability grouping and acceleration on K–12 students' academic achievement: Findings of two second-order meta-analyses. *Review of Educational Research, 86*(4), 849–899.

Stern, J., Ferraro, K., & Mohnkern, J. (2017). *Tools for teaching conceptual understanding, secondary: Designing lessons and assessments for deep learning*. Corwin.

Tanner, L. (1997). *Dewey's laboratory school: Lessons for today*. Teachers College Press.

Tapscott, D. (1998). *Growing up digital: The rise of the net generation*. McGraw-Hill.

The Hub.Community. (2020). *Home*. https://thehub.community

The New Teacher Project. (2018). *The opportunity myth: What students can show us about how school is letting them down and how to fix it*. https://tntp.org/assets/documents/TNTP_The-Opportunity-Myth_Web.pdf

Thiel Foundation. (2011). The Thiel Fellowship. https://thielfellowship.org

Trilling, B., & Fadel, C. (2009). *21st century skills: Learning for life in our times*. John Wiley & Sons.

Tucker, B. (2012). The flipped classroom. *Education Next, 12*(1), 82–83.

Tucker, C. R. (2020). *Balance with blended learning: Partner with your students to reimagine learning and reclaim your life*. Corwin.

Turkle, S. (1995). *Life on the screen: Identity in the age of the Internet*. Simon & Schuster.

Tyack, D., & Cuban, L. (1995). *Tinkering toward utopia: A century of public school reform*. Harvard University Press.

Tyack, D., & Tobin, W. (1994). The "grammar" of schooling: Why has it been so hard to change? *American Educational Research Journal, 31*(3), 453–479.

United Nations. (1989). *Convention on the Rights of the Child*. https://www.unicef.org/child-rights-convention/convention-text

United Nations. (2020, August). Policy brief: Education during COVID-19 and beyond. https://www.un.org/development/desa/dspd/wp-content/uploads/sites/22/2020/08/sg_policy_brief_covid-19_and_education_august_2020.pdf

University of Chicago Laboratory Schools. (n.d.). *About Lab*. https://www.ucls.uchicago.edu/about-lab

Veenman, S. (1995). Cognitive and noncognitive effects of multi-grade and multi-age classes: A best-evidence synthesis. *Review of Educational Research, 65*(4), 319–381. doi:10.3102/00346543065004319

Veenman, S. (1996). Effects of multigrade and multi-age classes reconsidered. *Review of Educational Research, 66*(3), 323–340. doi:10.3102/00346543066003323

Wagner, T. (2008). *The global achievement gap: Why even our best schools don't teach the new survival skills our children need—and what we can do about it*. Basic Books.

Wagner, T., & Dintersmith, T. (2016). *Most likely to succeed: Preparing our kids for the innovation era*. Scribner.

Walker, K. (2020, July 13). A digital jobs program to help America's economic recovery. *Grow With Google*. https://blog.google/outreach-initiatives/grow-with-google/digital-jobs-program-help-americas-economic-recovery

Wehmeyer, M., & Zhao, Y. (2020). *Teaching students to become self-determined learners*. ASCD.

World Economic Forum. (2020, October). *The Future of Jobs Report 2020*. http://www3.weforum.org/docs/WEF_Future_of_Jobs_2020.pdf

Yong Zhao. (2020, October 3). *Silver lining for learning | Episode 29* [Video]. YouTube. https://www.youtube.com/watch?v=SRJYS3NJCRU

Zhao, Y. (2009). *Catching up or leading the way: American education in the age of globalization*. ASCD.

Zhao, Y. (2011). Students as change partners: A proposal for educational change in the age of globalization. *Journal of Educational Change, 12*(2), 267–279. doi:10.1007/s10833-011-9159-9

Zhao, Y. (2012). *World class learners: Educating creative and entrepreneurial students*. Corwin.

Zhao, Y. (2016). From deficiency to strength: Shifting the mindset about education inequality. *Journal of Social Issues, 72*(4), 716–735.

Zhao, Y. (2017). What works can hurt: Side effects in education. *Journal of Educational Change, 18*(1), 1–19.

Zhao, Y. (2018a). The changing context of teaching and implications for teacher education. *Peabody Journal of Education, 93*(3), 295–308. https://doi.org/10.1080/0161956X.2018.1449896

Zhao, Y. (2018b). Personalizable education for greatness. *Kappa Delta Pi Record, 54*(3), 109–115.

Zhao, Y. (2018c). *Reach for greatness: Personalizable education for all children*. Corwin.

Zhao, Y. (2018d). The rise of the useless: The case for talent diversity. *Journal of Science Education and Technology, 28*, 62–68. https://doi.org/10.1007/s10956-018-9743-3

Zhao, Y. (2018e). *What works may hurt: Side effects in education*. Teachers College Press.

Zhao, Y. (2020a). COVID-19 as a catalyst for educational change. *Prospects, 49*, 29–33. doi:10.1007/s11125-020-09477-y

Zhao, Y. (2020b). Social learning and learning to be social: From online instruction to online education. *American Journal of Education, 127*(1), 137–142. https://doi.org/10.1086/711017

Zhao, Y. (2020c). Tofu is not cheese: Rethinking education amid the COVID-19 pandemic. *East China Normal University Review of Education, 3*(2), 189–203.

Zhao, Y. (2020d). Two decades of havoc: A synthesis of criticism against PISA. *Journal of Educational Change, 21*, 245–266. https://doi.org/10.1007/s10833-019-09367-x

Zhao, Y., Emler, T. E., Snethen, A., & Yin, D. (2019). *An education crisis is a terrible thing to waste: How radical changes can spark student excitement and success.* Teachers College Press.

Zhao, Y., & Tavangar, H. S. (2016). *World class learners: Personalized education for autonomous learning and student-driven curriculum.* Corwin.

Zhao, Y., Wehmeyer, M., Basham, J., & Hansen, D. (2019). Tackling the wicked problem of measuring what matters: Framing the questions. *East China Normal University Review of Education, 2*(3), 262–278. https://doi.org/10.1177%2F2096531119878965

Zhao, Y., Zhang, G., Lei, J., & Qiu, W. (2015). *Never send a human to do a machine's job: Correcting the top 5 edtech mistakes.* Corwin.

Index

Leadership That Makes an Impact

MICHAEL FULLAN & MARY JEAN GALLAGHER

With the goal of transforming the culture of learning to develop greater equity, excellence, and student well-being, this book will help you liberate the system and maintain focus.

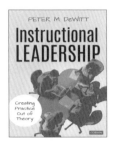

PETER M. DEWITT

This step-by-step how-to guide presents the six driving forces of instructional leadership within a multistage model for implementation, delivering lasting improvement through small collaborative changes.

BRYAN GOODWIN

If you've ever wondered anything, really—just out of curiosity—then you have what it takes to lead your school to restored curiosity and your students to well-being and success.

JOHN HATTIE & RAYMOND L. SMITH

Based on the most current Visible Learning® research with contributions from education thought leaders around the world, this book includes practical ideas for leaders to implement high-impact strategies to strengthen entire school cultures and advocate for all students.

DAVIS CAMPBELL & MICHAEL FULLAN

The model outlined in this book develops a systems approach to governing local schools collaboratively to become exemplars of highly effective decision-making, leadership, and action.

MICHAEL FULLAN, JOANNE QUINN, & JOANNE MCEACHEN

The comprehensive strategy of deep learning incorporates practical tools and processes to engage educational stakeholders in new partnerships, mobilize whole-system change, and transform learning for all students.

JOANNE QUINN, JOANNE MCEACHEN, MICHAEL FULLAN, MAG GARDNER, & MAX DRUMMY

Dive into deep learning with this hands-on guide to creating learning experiences that give purpose, unleash student potential, and transform not only learning, but life itself.

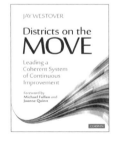

JAY WESTOVER

The transformative framework outlined in this book creates a districtwide approach for changing the culture of learning and creating a coherent system of continuous improvement.

CORWIN
A SAGE Publishing Company

Helping educators make the greatest impact

CORWIN HAS ONE MISSION: to enhance education through intentional professional learning.

We build long-term relationships with our authors, educators, clients, and associations who partner with us to develop and continuously improve the best evidence-based practices that establish and support lifelong learning.